Home Office Research Study 260

One problem among many: drug use among care leavers in transition to independent living

Jenni Ward, Zoë Henderson and Geoffrey Pearson
Public Policy Research Unit, Goldsmiths College, University of London

The views expressed in this report are those of the authors, not necessarily those of the Home Office (nor do they reflect Government policy).

Home Office Research, Development and Statistics Directorate
February 2003

Home Office Research Studies

The Home Office Research Studies are reports on research undertaken by or on behalf of the Home Office. They cover the range of subjects for which the Home Secretary has responsibility. Other publications produced by the Research, Development and Statistics Directorate include Findings, Statistical Bulletins and Statistical Papers.

The Research, Development and Statistics Directorate

RDS is part of the Home Office. The Home Office's purpose is to build a safe, just and tolerant society in which the rights and responsibilities of individuals, families and communities are properly balanced and the protection and security of the public are maintained.

RDS is also part of National Statistics (NS). One of the aims of NS is to inform Parliament and the citizen about the state of the nation and provide a window on the work and performance of government, allowing the impact of government policies and actions to be assessed.

Therefore –

Research Development and Statistics Directorate exists to improve policy making, decision taking and practice in support of the Home Office purpose and aims, to provide the public and Parliament with information necessary for informed debate and to publish information for future use.

First published 2003
Application for reproduction should be made to the Communications and Development Unit, Room 201, Home Office, 50 Queen Anne's Gate, London SW1H 9AT.
© Crown copyright 2003   ISBN 1 84082 957.5
ISSN 0072 6435

Foreword

This report is one of five research reports published as part of the Vulnerable Groups Research Programme. The central focus of the programme was to investigate patterns of drug use among groups of vulnerable young people and their access to services. Each project focuses on a different group of vulnerable young people, who tend not to be included in general population surveys. The project reported on here concentrates on young people leaving care including runaways. The four other projects examine: young people involved in sex work; homeless young people; young drug users who are in contact with drugs services; and young people in contact with youth offending teams. Many of the young people across these projects are likely to have had similar backgrounds and vulnerabilities. A number of the studies explore this area and the degree to which the young people are in fact the same population caught at different points in their lives and via different services.

The main aim of this study is to examine the way in which care leavers' drug use developed during the process of their leaving state care to live independently. Care leavers face the challenge of setting up and managing a home, getting a job, coping financially and developing a support network at a very young age. The Children (leaving care) Act 2000 placed a new responsibility on social services to assist care leavers in this transition to independent living, beyond the age of 16. For a variety of reasons – adverse childhood experiences, a high incidence of psychological and behavioural problems and feelings of loss and fragmentation following time in care – young care leavers are considered particularly vulnerable to having or developing drug problems. Where drug use may have become established while living in state care, risky patterns of drug use may develop as a young person moves towards independence. To date, little research has focused on care leavers and their drug use. This study begins to fill this gap and proposes some areas where drugs services for young care leavers could be improved.

Tom Bucke
Programme Director, Drugs and Alcohol Research
Research, Development and Statistics Directorate
Home Office
2003

Acknowledgments

The authors wish to express thanks to all those who assisted us in completing our study. These included a number of people employed within leaving care teams of social service departments, staff in foyer projects who assisted us to contact young people and accommodated our demands within their busy working schedules.

Our particular thanks go to the young people who agreed to be interviewed as part of the study.

Jenni Ward
Zoë Henderson
Geoffrey Pearson

The authors

Jenni Ward is a senior researcher at the Public Policy Research Unit, Goldsmiths College, University of London.

Zoë Henderson was the research assistant for 12 months working on this research with Jenni Ward.

Geoffrey Pearson is a professor in the Professional and Community Education Department, Goldsmiths College, University of London.

Researchers working in Drugs and Alcohol Research at the Home Office would like to thank the independent assessor for this report.

Contents

Summary

Introduction and background

This 12-month study (July 2001 to June 2002), funded by the Home Office Drugs and Alcohol Research Unit, examined young care leavers' patterns of drug use as they moved from care to live independently. Young people who had left the parental home at a young age (so-called 'runaways') were also included in the study.

It is well known that young people with a history of state care are vulnerable to a series of poor life outcomes. While drug use is often included in the list of disadvantages, to date little research has focused on drug use among care leavers, specifically.

The study employed both quantitative and qualitative research methods.

Methods

(i) A survey was conducted with 200 young people in the process of leaving care, or having recently left care, on their experiences with drugs, including alcohol and tobacco, together with other lifestyle and health issues.

(ii) A sub-sample of 30 were selected to participate in an in-depth interview on their experiences of care and leaving care, with a focus on recent changes in their progress towards independent living and associated changes in patterns of drug use. These interviews were carried out six months after the first interview contact.

Findings

The sample consisted of young people aged 13-24 years, average age 18 years.

Summary findings are as follows:

- High levels of self-reported drug use compared with general population surveys.

- Mainly cannabis use. Almost three-quarters (73%) have smoked it, one-half (52%) in the last month, and a third (34%) reporting that they smoke it daily.

- One-tenth had used cocaine within the last month. Fifteen per cent have used ecstasy within the month, reflecting the involvement of this age group in the modern dance club culture.

- The use of heroin and crack cocaine both reported around ten per cent lifetime prevalence.

- Little difference was found in drug use between young men and women.

- Young black people were less likely to use drugs (44% had not taken any drug) compared with 82 per cent of young white people who had. Among those of mixed parentage 95 per cent had taken an illicit drug at some point in their lives.

- Two-thirds of the sample (67%) reported that they were daily cigarette smokers. The average age at which smoking began was 13 years of age, with individual ages ranged from seven to twenty years.

- Alcohol consumption was considerably lower, most drinking at least once a week (34%), at least once a month (20%), or less than once a month (23%). Fifteen per cent reported that they had either never drunk alcohol, or had stopped, and nine per cent reported that they drank alcohol most days.

Qualitative interview outcomes

- Steadily lower levels of drug consumption were reported as young people assumed/ approached independent living status.

- Increasing levels were reported during periods of transition in hostels, attributable to peer-group influences, and among those whose movement to independent living was premature or poorly planned.

- Practical responsibilities such as household management, when well planned as part of the care leaving transition encourage more responsible levels of drug consumption.

- Similarly, for the small number who had become parents, childcare responsibilities were an encouragement to more stable lifestyles.

- 'Maturing out' of drug use occurs at a younger age for young care leavers than that found within the general population.

Support and service provision

- Where the denial of a drug problem is a barrier to receiving help, not knowing how or where to seek help is also a barrier.

- Young people leaving the family home at a young age to survive on their own were at greater risk of drug and alcohol problems than young care leavers. These young people were found to be at risk of slipping through the net in terms of escaping the authorities' attention as a group in need of appropriate help and intervention with drug-related issues in particular.

- Approaches, which work with the overlapping aspects of young care leavers' lives (holistic approaches), are responded to with more enthusiasm than single-need approaches.

- Whereas drugs prevention education might seem to be an anomaly with a group of young people whose drug use was already established, education focusing on resisting pressure from others to use drugs or to resist progressing on to other forms of drug use, maybe of benefit.

- Where hostels and foyer project accommodation adopt a 'zero tolerance' policy to drug use, this should not preclude the need to pass on simple drugs prevention messages, including harm reduction measures.

- A young care leaver's sense of self-worth and self-esteem should be encouraged and promoted (this might include validating the care leaver's 'drug wise' evaluation of drug risks).

Recommendations: policy and practice

- This study has confirmed a lack of appropriate specialist services for young people with drug problems.

- Even so, social services are the lead agency in assisting young care leavers with transition issues, including drug problems. Staff, therefore, need to be adequately prepared to respond to drug-related issues.

- Drugs were only a small part of the challenges these young people faced on leaving care. Any interventions should be part of more general planning, embracing issues such as housing, employment and training based on a comprehensive needs assessment.

1   Introduction: background and methods

Political changes to the status of care leavers: New legislation in context

It is generally well recognised that young people with a state care background[1] are a very vulnerable and disadvantaged group of individuals (Broad, 1999; Buchanan, 1999; Blyth, 2001; Lewis, 2000; Valios, 2001). It is also well recognised that this particular cross-section of young people have very specific needs that must be met in order to ensure a smooth transition into independent adulthood. For example, it has been estimated that up to 50 per cent of care leavers are unemployed with as many as 75 per cent having no formal educational qualifications and that up to 20 per cent experience some kind of homelessness within two years of leaving care. Furthermore, 23 per cent of adult prisoners and 38 per cent of young prisoners are care leavers (Department of Health, 1999). Also, it has been found that young people from state care backgrounds are much more likely to run away than those young people who have not been in state care (Social Exclusion Unit, 2001 and Broad, 1999). This results in their living and surviving on the streets by way of thieving or selling their bodies.

The process of young people leaving state care has significantly changed in recent years. A number of government initiatives and legislative changes recently set in place have had direct implications on the quality of life experienced by young care leavers. The initiatives were initially introduced as a way of increasing support for those who depend on the state to act as their legal guardians. In 1998 funding of £885 million was used to mark care leaving services as a priority under the 'Quality Protects Programme' that aimed to "improve the life chances of young people in and leaving local authority care" (Department of Health, 2000). In conjunction with the government's Social Exclusion Unit, a move was made to ensure that "all young persons leaving care, as they enter adulthood, are not isolated and participate socially and economically as citizens" (Department of Health, 2000). In order for those with a state care background to be fully integrated into playing a participating role in wider society, the government recognised that an extension of adolescent support services was required.

Before the introduction of the Children (Leaving Care) Act 2000, it was not compulsory for Social Services to assist young care leavers beyond the age of 16. Although some local authorities did have leaving care services in place, from 16 years onwards, young care

---

1   A state care background refers to young people who had been accommodated in both residential and foster care. Although the vast majority (65-70%) of young people living in state care are accommodated in foster care, it is common for young people to spend periods of time both in foster care placements and residential care homes.

leavers were often left to fend for themselves in all the challenging aspects of life, such as securing employment and a place to live. Recent research has pointed to the increasingly complex set of tasks and routes that must be traversed by young people in modern Britain as they attain young adult status (Furlong and Cartmel, 1997; Economic and Social Research Council, 2002).

These challenges are particularly difficult for young people with a care background, given the depressing life chances they have so often experienced and their reduced 'social capital'. For example, Vernon (2000) notes that care leavers face an accelerated transition into independence. They are forced to live independently, tackle the multiple challenges of managing a home, find and remain in employment, cope financially and build and sustain a network of support and friendships, all within a very short space of time. These challenges are set against the backdrop of care leavers being a disadvantaged group.

Furthermore, these challenges have to be faced at a much younger age than their peers in wider society who on average leave home at 22 years of age and typically come from more stable and supportive backgrounds. However, new legislation has extended the local authorities' responsibilities to provide accommodation and financial assistance to 17- and 18-year-olds, who have been in care for at least 13 weeks at some point in the two years before their 16th birthday. Further support is provided for any care leaver remaining in full-time higher education up to 21 years of age, to encourage educational attainment and improve their chances of employment.

These recent changes to the legal system within the United Kingdom are partly based on ideas practised in the United States (Collins, 2001). More specifically, the newly established leaving care teams within social services departments, and the general ethos behind UK Government foyer projects are somewhat akin to 'Independent Living Programmes' and 'Transitional Living Programmes' that operate in other countries. These programmes offer life skills training to care leavers and young people from non-state care backgrounds who have little, if any familial support. The independent living programmes specifically target state care leavers. The transitional living programmes essentially target support services at homeless youths aged between 16 and 21, not in the custody of state child welfare systems, though many of their users have been in state care.

Similar initiatives have been set up in the United Kingdom: foyer projects have been operating successfully since the mid-1990s to assist young people aged between 16 and 25 from disadvantaged and/or homeless backgrounds. A large number of service users have care backgrounds. At the time of writing there were 139 projects operating across England,

Scotland and Wales, which provide young people with resources and support as they make the transition into adulthood and independence. A strong emphasis is placed on promoting education and training, as in the newly established leaving care teams.

Since the introduction of the Children (Leaving Care) Act 2000 procedures for assisting care leavers into their future independence have been formalised in a similar way to the United States where the federal government funds formal, written 'transitional independent living plans'. In the UK, there is what is known as a 'pathway plan' that involves mapping out a young person's future in a holistic way. This plan is pivotal to the process of articulating a young person's aspirations and identifying interim goals to help them realise their ambitions. A pathway plan is set in place before a young person is due to leave care. It is designed to specify the type of help the young person will be receiving, and incorporate contingency arrangements in the event of a breakdown, for instance, in the young person's living arrangements. New government legislation aims to promote effective pathway planning so that it can be used to gauge whether young people are ready to leave care or not, and what work remains to be done to ensure leaving care occurs with as few problems as possible.

The theory behind the introduction of the pathway plan was based on research findings that young people who leave care with incomplete life skills tend to fare worse in adjusting to a life of independence. Indeed, the Children (Leaving Care) Act 2000 document notes that "most young people experience difficulties and the occasional crisis during their journey to adulthood, but they are usually able to return home and often have a wide network of support to help them get back on their feet. Young people leaving care, whose lives have not been easy, may lack these supports and yet be expected to cope with major changes in their lives, often at a younger age than other young people" (Department of Health, 2000). It is therefore of crucial importance that potential crises are foreseen and contingency arrangements are built into the pathway planning process, being both sensitive and flexible to the lifestyles of young care leavers.

Care leavers and drug use

Illegal drugs and their use is an issue that affects the lives of every young person in Britain today. This is whether a young person is merely offered drugs, becomes tempted to experiment in using illegal substances as a natural part of their adolescent curiosity, or if drug use develops into more serious and established patterns of use that can lead to dependency and behaviour disorders. Despite their illegality, drugs remain readily available and are easily accessible for relatively cheap prices in comparison to market prices of the past (Home Office, 2000).

Historically, it has been widely noted that young people who have grown up in state care are particularly vulnerable to developing or having substance misuse problems (Biehal *et al.*, 1995; Social Services Inspectorate, 1997). Care leavers' vulnerability to drug use can be seen to exist for a range of reasons. A number of studies have emphasised the high incidence of psychological and behavioural problems among young people who live in care. These result from both pre-care experiences and the negative effect of living in care (Colton *et al.*, 1991; Hendricks, 1989; McCann *et al.*, 1996; Social Services Inspectorate, 1997 as cited in Ward, 1998).

Indeed, Ward (1998) suggested that care homes provide 'ready made peer groups' that can increase the chances of peer pressure in relation to trying out illegal substances, added to pressure of fulfilling a need to feel part of a substitute family group after experiencing breakdowns within their own home environments. Where drug use may have become established while living in state care, risky drug using patterns of behaviour may develop as a young person exits from the system to live independently. To date, little research exists that has focused on care leavers as a specific group of young people and their drug use patterns as they move towards independence. This study aimed to do just this. The research was carried out over a 12-month period between July 2001 and June 2002.

Aims and objectives of the study

The main aim of the research was to examine the way in which drug use developed alongside the process of leaving state care to live independently. Young people, who had left the parental home, at a young age and typically under conflict situations, were also included in the study. The reason for including this latter group was that an earlier study carried out with young people living in state care identified a blurring of lines between 'young runaways' and young care leavers. Where young runaways usually relied upon the support of friends and friends' families at the point of running away, it was not common for them to require Social Services interventions further down the line.

From a policy perspective young runaways and young care leavers are treated as two distinct groups. However, there is an overlap in that they both become independent at a young age and given the often-troubled backgrounds they come from, they are usually negotiating their independence alongside low levels of family support. It is rare for young people who flee the family home in the older adolescent years to experience a successful reunification with the family (Bullock *et al.*, 1998). For the purpose of this report the two groups are referred to as young care leavers.

Methods

The study employed both quantitative and qualitative research methods. A self-report survey was conducted with 200 young people who were being prepared to leave the care system and young people who had recently left care or the family home to live on their own. A sub-sample of 30 young people were selected from the 200 and participated in an in-depth tape-recorded interview, six months after the first interview contact.

Self-report survey

In order to compare the study's findings with some of the statistics reported on young care leavers, the survey collected a range of information though a key focus was to measure the prevalence of illegal drug use. Respondents were accessed mainly through leaving care teams of social services departments and foyer projects in addition to some being recruited from homeless (night) shelters and YMCA centres. Staff members employed within these services and projects were asked to assist the recruitment of young people to the study.

The criteria for inclusion in this part of the study were that the young person was either being prepared to leave the care system to live independently or had made the move to independence in the past few years. This was to capture young people who were in the process of becoming independent.

The survey was conducted using a structured questionnaire. A researcher completed each questionnaire in a face-to-face interview with the young person. This approach safeguarded against issues to do with illiteracy and gave the young person more confidence surrounding confidentiality. It was also useful in that a relationship could be built up. This was helpful when contacting young people again six months later to participate in the in-depth interviews.

A reliability check was in place, in that an honesty-test question in relation to drug use was included. Reliability was assumed to be high as not one respondent claimed to have taken the fake drug included in the list of drugs. This was reassuring in the light of knowing that self-report data also run the risk of over-reporting as well as under-reporting, due to bravado or the pressure to conform to perceived peer norms. A further, albeit somewhat informal, check on the reliability of responses was that leaving care staff often verified those young people with more serious drug use issues in advance.

The questionnaire was designed on a similar model to one used previously with similar aged young people. Specifically it used a language relevant to the young people being questioned (see Appendix A). Revisions to the initial questionnaire were made following a pilot with ten young people.

Given the tight timeframe of the study it was necessary to impose an opportunistic sampling frame whereby those young people who were using the services or were present in the hostel on the day of the survey, providing they fitted the selection criteria, were invited to participate.

In-depth interviews

The interview explored the specific ways in which drug use had developed or changed alongside young people's move from the care system to live independently (see Appendix B). Selection of this sub-sample for the in-depth interview was based on a range of criteria. Overall a purposive sampling frame was used.

Of prime importance was to include young people who had recently made the move from care or the family home to live independently. This was to assess whether the shift in status to becoming independent had in any way impacted on their use of drugs. In addition the sub-sample was chosen to include a range of drug use experiences; young people who used drugs in a relatively minor way and those who were more dependent upon them. It was also important that the sub-sample reflected the larger sample in terms of age, gender and area location.

A few other factors affected the selection process. Some young people expressed they were not willing to be contacted again at a later date. Also it was necessary to consider whether a young person would be able to cope with the demands of a detailed interview which would raise sensitive issues in regard to their current and past lives.

Staff interviews

A series of focused interviews were also carried out with 15 staff members employed in the services, which helped facilitate access to young people. This included staff employed within social services leaving care teams and staff employed in housing and homeless agencies. These interviews explored the type of drug-related issues that were presented to them in their different support roles and the type of responses they made (see Appendix C). Those selected for interview reflected the range of personnel working with young care leavers. The different employment status of those interviewed is laid out in Table 1.1 and staff perceptions of the young people with whom they were working have been addressed in Chapter 4.

Table 1.1: **Interviews with leaving care team personnel and others**

Staff	No. of interviews
Senior social workers/managers	3
Social workers	6
Housing/homeless agency staff	5
Specialist drugs/alcohol worker	1
Total	15

Ethical approval

For research with vulnerable groups such as young people leaving care ethical considerations are of the utmost importance, to ensure confidentiality and protect other interests of these young people. The proposal was scrutinised by the appropriate Ethical Committee of Goldsmiths College, and the proposal also had to be agreed by the Association of Directors of Social Services (ADSS) in order to authorise access. The researchers had already conducted a two-year study of drug use among young people in care, funded by the Economic and Social Research Council, and so were already familiar with the requirements of ADSS and other sensitive issues of approach and access involved in research of this kind.

Characteristics of the survey sample

The sample of care leavers was aged between 14 and 24 years with an average age of 18. The specific age breakdown is presented in Table 1.2 and, as is indicated, the vast majority was aged between 16 and 21. Just over half were male (56%) which closely reflects the figures reported in the official statistics of young people accommodated in state care (Department of Health, 2002). Nearly three-fifths (59%) were white. Just under a third (28%) were black and a further ten per cent were mixed race. The remaining three per cent were of Asian, Oriental, South American and Eastern European descent.

Table 1.2: Age of respondents

Age of respondents	%
Under 16	3.5
16-18	59.0
19-21	29.5
Over 21	8.0
Total	100

Note: One young person was aged 14.
        Base n=200.

In order to represent a broad population range, young people were accessed from four main geographic locations, illustrated in Table 1.3.

Table 1.3: Regional location of the sample

Region	%
London	45
Merseyside	15
West Country	12
South East England	28

Note: The London sub-sample includes both inner city and outer London borough areas.
        Base n=200.

Care backgrounds

The study included young people who had both been in care and young people who had left the family home at a young age, so-called 'runaways'. Almost three-quarters (72%) of the sample had a care background and indeed 20 per cent were still 'in care' at the point of completing the questionnaire. The rest (28%) were early home-leavers. This latter group is important in that they, although a vulnerable group, had to date received little attention (Bedell, 2001). Moreover, this study suggests that they are in many ways more 'at risk' than the care leavers.

Accommodation status

Table 1.4 illustrates the type of accommodation respondents were living in at the point of completing the questionnaire. There are a variety of accommodation types available to young care leavers. This varies across the country and in many ways is connected to local provision and the way different local authorities organise themselves. As with anyone, young care leavers differ in their levels of coping and resilience; some are more ready for responsible living arrangements, such as occupying their own flats, than others. Furthermore, there is a (limited) degree of choice in accommodation type at this time point and some prefer the more supported type, despite the rules and curfews imposed.

Table 1.4 Accommodation type of survey respondents

Accommodation type	%
Own flats/bedsits (alone or with others)	22
Supported lodgings/foyer projects	37
Social services care placement	11
Hostels (including B&B's)	24
No fixed abode	6
Total	100

Note: No fixed abode refers to people who were sleeping rough or sleeping on a friend's floor.
         Base n=200.

Employment status
Confirming the statistics noted in the introduction, just half of the young people questioned (50%) were involved in formal education or training, variously attending school, college, or university and a small proportion (9%) were in full-time employment. This level of engagement might however involve some over-reporting, in that a number alluded to their limited attendance and interest in the courses and training programmes on which they were registered. A third (34%) were registered unemployed or were currently not doing anything and the remaining seven per cent were on sickness benefit, or currently expecting or looking after a baby.

Offending history
A substantial rate of incarceration for previous criminal offending was found in the sample. A total of nine per cent of respondents (7% male and 2% female) reported having lived in a secure setting or Young Offenders Institute (YOI) in the past and one respondent was in prison at the point of the follow-up interview. The majority of those who had lived in a secure setting/YOI had done so on only one occasion (n=11), but five had done so on two occasions and the remaining two had been in secure units on at least five occasions or more. The length of time spent in a secure environment ranged from one month to three

years with an average period of 2.5 months. These findings are in line with general statistics on the poor life outcomes of care leavers.

General health

All respondents were asked to describe their general health. Over three-quarters (77%) rated themselves as being in either excellent, very good or good health but almost a quarter (23%) said their health was either fair or poor. Reasons given for poor health were related mainly to diet and illness, including suffering depression, asthma, alcoholism, and complaints due to sleeping rough. Prescribed medication was being taken by a fifth (21%) of respondents. The most common reason for being prescribed medication was for depression, which sadly affected eight per cent of the total sample. These results were supportive of those found in a study into the health care needs of young people leaving care conducted in Surrey (Saunders and Broad, 1997). This study found that 17 per cent of its sample (n=48) had long-term mental health issues that largely included depression, and that 31 per cent had been referred, or had referred themselves, for medical help.

Parenthood

Although the majority (86%) of the sample did not have any children of their own, ten per cent had one child at the time of completing the questionnaire or were expecting a baby in the near future, and four per cent had two or more children. These patterns were in sharp contrast with those for the British population as a whole. According to the Teenage Pregnancy Unit at the Department of Health (1998) only three per cent of young women aged 15 to 19 had given birth in 1998.

In Chapter 2 findings from the survey are presented. As has been already noted, there is a dearth of reliable evidence on the nature and extent of drug use among young people growing up within the care system and those who have recently left it. This is the focus of the next chapter.

2　　Patterns of substance use among care leavers

In addition to recording past and current drug using patterns among the sample, the self-report survey was designed to collect information on the relative views of drug harm as well as familial substance using patterns. Information on experiences and views of cigarette smoking and alcohol consumption was also included. Findings on each of these behaviours are presented in turn.

Cigarette smoking

The majority (67%) were daily cigarette smokers and had been smoking since on average 13 years of age, although some had started as young as seven. The number of cigarettes smoked in a day ranged from one to 60. Ten was the average number smoked. Eight per cent had never smoked and a further fifth (19%) smoked in the past but had since given up. The remaining few (6%) claimed to be occasional smokers choosing to smoke only once or less in a week. There were no significant differences between the number of men and women who smoked and the amount of cigarettes smoked.

The majority of respondents believed cigarette smoking to be either 'fairly' (35%) or 'very' harmful (27%) compared with 26 per cent and nine per cent who viewed smoking as 'not very' and 'not at all' harmful respectively. A minority (3%) were either not sure, or believed it depended on the quantity that were smoked. Interestingly, no significant differences in the views of harmfulness were found to exist between those who smoked and those who did not. Both smokers and non-smokers equally rated smoking to be either 'very' or 'fairly' harmful suggesting that those young people who smoked cigarettes did so with informed knowledge about the negative consequences for their general health.

The levels of smoking by both men and women in the study seemed to be much higher than that found in previous studies involving general population surveys. Miller and Plant's (1996) survey of the drinking, smoking and drug use patterns of 7,722 15 and 16-year-olds found that 67 per cent had smoked at some point in their lives and just over a third of the sample had smoked in the last 30 days. The high levels of smoking found in the current study could be explained by a factor Foster and colleagues (1990) noted, that individuals who lived with their parents were less likely to smoke than those who were living away from the parental home.

Patterns of alcohol consumption

Table 2.1 illustrates how frequently the young people consumed alcohol. The majority were social drinkers who drank on a weekly basis or less. A small proportion had experimented with alcohol but had since ceased to drink and a few claimed to never having tried drinking. Where the majority of those who drank were social drinkers nearly half (48%) said they drank five or more drinks in a typical drinking session. As well, it is important to draw attention to the nine per cent who were heavy drinkers, who drank most days and whose patterns of drinking involved consuming at least five drinks or more in a typical drinking session.

A similar pattern was revealed in Miller and Plant's (1996) study, whereby half (50%) of the sample had consumed five or more drinks in a single drinking session in the last 30 days and the same proportion had been intoxicated in the same time period. Those who reported heavy drinking in the current study were equally as likely to be male or female. The average age of onset for drinking alcohol on a regular basis was 15 years. Drinking on a regular basis was defined as the point at which they had begun purchasing alcohol either alone or with peers, for their own consumption.

Table 2.1: Frequency of alcohol consumption among respondents

Frequency of alcohol consumption	%
Drink alcohol most days	9
Drink alcohol at least once a week	34
Drink alcohol at least once a month	20
Drink alcohol less than once a month	23
Used to drink alcohol but don't drink now	10
Never drink alcohol	4
Total	100

Note: Base n=200.

Views of alcohol harm

All of the young people were asked how harmful they viewed drinking alcohol to be. The majority believed it to be 'fairly' (37%) or 'very' (26%) harmful in contrast to those who thought it was 'not very' (24%) or 'not at all' (6%) harmful. The remaining few (7%) were either unsure or stated that 'it depended how much was consumed'.

It was surprising that nearly a third (30%) believed alcohol to be 'not very harmful' or 'not at all harmful', although this was very much in line with the attitudes of young people generally as indicated by the research on public attitudes conducted on behalf of the Independent Inquiry into the Misuse of Drugs Act (Police Foundation, 2000; Pearson and Shiner, 2002). The dangers associated with alcohol have been recognised by Rutter et al., (1998), cited in Newburn and Shiner (2001), who stated: "considered in population terms, alcohol is a more important risk factor for antisocial behaviour than are other drugs because it is more frequently taken in excess" (p. 154). The sample population here then were to some extent vulnerable to alcohol-related risk and harm when it was considered one-third continued to drink alcohol at least once a week and a tenth drank to get drunk at least three or four times a week, if not everyday.

A discrepancy in the views of harm was found between those who were either non-drinkers or social drinkers and those who reported problematic drinking behaviours. The majority of non-social drinkers believed alcohol consumption to be 'very' or 'fairly' harmful, a view in contrast to that of problematic drinkers, the majority of whom rated it as being 'not very' or 'not at all' harmful. This finding suggests that those young people who were at risk from their patterns of heavy and regular drinking appeared to be unaware or perhaps even in denial of the harm to which they were exposing themselves. Consistent with this assumption are findings presented by Plant et al., (1990), who found that young heavy drinkers were more inclined than other teenagers to give 'positive' reasons for drinking.

Family alcohol consumption

When respondents were asked about drinking by family members, the majority claimed their parents were socially moderate or light drinkers. However, it was found that ten per cent of mothers and 17 per cent of fathers were described as heavy drinkers who drank everyday, and in most of these cases the label 'alcoholic' was added. Four per cent came from a family where both parents were described as heavy drinkers. In respect of heavy parental drinking, it was often alluded that this was the reason for their entering the care system in the first place.

Of those who were from a family where one or both parents drank heavily, a quarter (25%) had themselves gone on to develop patterns of heavy drinking and on a slightly different slant seven per cent had become 'problematic' drug users[2]. Support for these

---

2   Problematic drug users as measured by the screening tool ASMA (Assessment of Substance Misuse in Adolescence). This is described in more detail under the illegal drugs section below.

findings comes from previous research which shows that family support, family control and family drinking styles have all been identified as having an important influence on young people's drinking. Low parental support and control and heavy parental drinking have been associated with heavy drinking by young people (Foxcroft and Lowe, 1991; Lowe *et al.*, 1993).

Changes in drinking patterns

To investigate changing patterns of substance use, respondents were asked about their drinking patterns over the last year compared to previous years. This revealed that, in the majority of cases, drinking levels remained relatively consistent or had decreased. Nine per cent had stopped drinking altogether. Just a quarter (26%) said they had been drinking more over the last year, so the overall trend appeared to be evenly split in terms of those who were consuming more or less alcohol.

Table 2.2:   **Respondents drinking patterns over the last year**

Drinking patterns over the last year	%
Drinking more	26
Drinking has stayed the same	31
Drinking less	29
Have stopped drinking	9
Never drink	5
Total	100

Note: Base n=200.

Reasons for stopping or at least cutting back ranged from: maturing and growing out of the need to drink; having changed living arrangements; a baby to look after or one on the way; or because of health problems. However, those who continued to drink and to do so more frequently said that this was due to having easier access to public houses, reaching the legal age to be served, or that they had a greater psychological need such as needing to relieve boredom, loneliness and depression. Others cited they were drinking more as a result of using drugs less frequently and a consequent need to fill the gap.

Some of the reasons for drinking alcohol were similar to those found in previous research studies into young peoples' drinking behaviours. For instance, Marsh *et al.*, (1986), noted that teenage alcohol consumption was largely incorporated into the development of identity.

Patterns of illegal drug use

Illegal drug use in this population was common. Three-quarters (75%) of the total sample reported past use, or were still using illegal drugs, compared to one-quarter (25%) who had never tried any drugs. This general finding supported results found in a previous study conducted by Newburn *et al.*, (2002). This earlier study looked at the illegal drug using patterns of young people living in state care. Here it was found that two-thirds of the sample had tried an illegal drug at some point in their lives. More specifically, in the present study, the smoking of cannabis was found to be commonplace with almost three-quarters (73%) of the total sample having 'ever' smoked it. The next most commonly used drugs were ecstasy and amphetamines, followed by cocaine, solvents, nitrites and LSD. Although having been tried by far smaller proportions, 14 per cent had tried crack cocaine and nine per cent had tried heroin.

Some of the young people reported frequent use of particular types of drugs. Cannabis smoking was by far the most popular form of drug use with just over half (52%) the total sample having smoked it within the last month. A third (34%) reported smoking cannabis everyday. This level of self-reported cannabis and other illicit drug use was considerably higher than among groups of young people of similar age sampled for the British Crime Survey and Parker's surveys conducted in the north west of England and elsewhere (Ramsay *et al.*, 2001; Parker *et al.*, 1998).

Ecstasy was the second most frequently used drug. As figure 2.1 illustrates, a significant number of the sample had used drugs such as ecstasy, cocaine, amphetamines and nitrites in the last year; which are drugs often associated with the nightclub scene. Whilst the regular use of crack cocaine and heroin was low, seven and five per cent had used these class A drugs within the last year. The decline in solvent use among respondents might support the notion that solvents are typically used in the earlier years of drug experimentation when accessibility to illicit drugs is somewhat more difficult for younger age groups than older ones in their late teens.

Figure 2.1:   Frequency of care leavers drug use

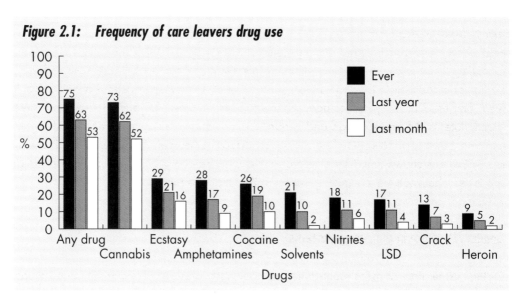

The findings in this study are generally consistent with other studies of similarly vulnerable young people (Evans and Alade, 2000, Goulden and Sondhi, 2001). However, if the figures are compared to young people recorded in the general population, the levels of use for all substances among this sample of young people were much higher. Figure 2.2 illustrates this by comparing drug use levels between the care leavers in this study and 16 to 18-year-old respondents in the year 2000 wave of the British Crime Survey. Attention is drawn to the sharpest difference, which is the greater propensity of the care leaver sample to have used Class A drugs, such as ecstasy, cocaine, crack and heroin.

Figure 2.2:   'Ever' drug use of care leavers and 16 to 18-year-olds in the British Crime Survey 2000

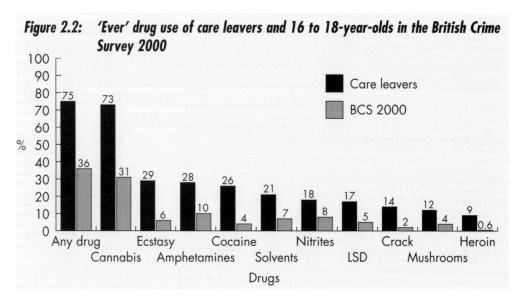

Age of first drug use

Exploring the age at which respondents in this study had first tried drugs revealed fairly similar patterns to that found in other youth surveys. On average cannabis and solvents were first used at 14 years of age. Amphetamines, nitrites, LSD and ecstasy were used slightly later at 15 years of age and heroin, cocaine and crack cocaine were tried slightly later, on average at 16 years of age. Research (Health Education Authority, 1999; Parker *et al.*, 1998) has shown that there is a progressive age trend at which specific types of drugs are taken. The results of this study generally reflect that age pattern.

Gender difference in drug using patterns

Of the 75 per cent of respondents who had previously used or were currently using drugs, just over half (55%) were men. This reflects the overall gender ratio of the sample. There were, however, some differences between the types of drugs used, though the differences were not significant. For example, whilst men and women were just as likely to smoke cannabis, women were slightly more likely to have used heroin. A further gender difference was that women were more likely to report having taken 'unknown pills', which could be linked to their higher incidence of pill overdose in attempted suicide than young men (Bradford and Urquhart, 1998).

Although the rate of suicide attempts among this sample was not systematically recorded, a number of young people alluded to having made a serious attempt in the past, and indeed two women participating in the in-depth interview described suicide attempts through paracetamol and other pill overdose. Furthermore, although the overall proportion of those having used magic mushrooms and ketamine were relatively small, men (71% and 67%) were more likely to have used them than women (29% and 33%).

Difference in drug using patterns by ethnicity

An analysis of drug use and preference by ethnicity revealed that young black people in the study (n=55) were more inclined not to use drugs, than to use them. This has been confirmed elsewhere (Ramsay and Spiller, 1997). Nearly half (44%) had not taken any drugs. Mixed race young people (n=19) on the other hand were more inclined to use drugs (95%) than not, as were young white people (n=118, 82%).

Difference in drug using patterns by care leavers and runaways

Although young runaways and young care leavers have been discussed as one group, if drug use among them is examined as two separate groups, young runaways had higher levels of use for almost all the drugs, though the difference was not significant. Figure 2.3 illustrates the levels of lifetime use among them. A similar pattern was revealed for more recent drug use such as use 'in the last year' and 'last month'.

Figure 2.3: Difference in lifetime drug use by young runaways and young care leavers

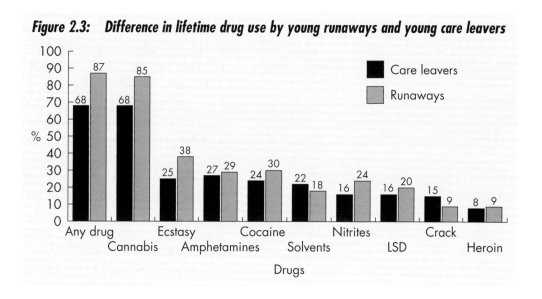

Views of drug harm

When asked how harmful specific drug types were, the majority of young people in the study viewed anything other than cannabis as 'very harmful'. Nearly half (45%) rated cannabis as being 'not very' harmful.

Table 2.3:   Views of drug harm

Drugs	'Very harmful'	'Fairly harmful'	'Not very harmful'	'Not at all harmful'	'Don't know'	Totals
Heroin	93	3	0	0	4	100
Cocaine	75	14	3	2	5	99
Ecstasy	66	25	2	0	6	99
Amphetamines	53	28	7	0	11	99
Cannabis	10	17	45	24	4	100

Note: Where a row does not total 100% a response 'depends' was given, which has not been included here.
Base =200.

There were more widespread views of harm in relation to using cannabis with a quarter (24%) saying that it was 'not at all harmful', 17 per cent 'fairly harmful' whilst the remaining four per cent were undecided. The tendency to see cannabis as considerably less harmful than other illicit drugs is not specific to care leavers, and similar results have been reported in other studies. In a survey of 16 to 59-year-olds, Pearson and Shiner (2002) found that cannabis was viewed as the least harmful of all drugs, including alcohol and tobacco, and also showed fundamental agreement between older teenagers and adults of all ages. No attempt was made to assess perceptions of drug harm among care workers employed by social services departments, so it is not known whether a similar convergence of views would have been found across the 'generation divide'.

Drug use and risk

In addition to exploring the regularity at which young people used drugs, the questionnaire contained several questions designed to ascertain the proportion of problematic drug use among the sample. To do this, the screening test called ASMA (Assessment of Substance Misuse in Adolescence), as developed by Swadi (1997) and later modified by Willner (2000), was used. The responses given to these questions were scaled and subsequently classified into one of five types of drug using behaviour. The results are displayed in Table 2.4. It is important to point out that although the assessment tool was useful, the measures were in some respects crude.

Without doubt the sample included a proportion of young people who were either at risk of developing serious problems with their drug use or who already had. However, the 'potentially problematic' category was too inclusive and risked a 'net-widening' effect.

Problematic drug use was defined as becoming addicted to heroin and/or crack cocaine. It could also include drug use which could be defined as chaotic in the sense that other aspects of the young person's life had fallen into decline as a result of drug use, such as becoming homeless or becoming involved in crime to fund the cost of drugs. A fifth (21%) of the sample were categorised as problematic.

Table 2.4:   Respondents' drug use as categorised by the ASMA screening tool

Categories	%
Non-user	29
Non-problematic	17
Potentially problematic	28
Problematic	21
Ex-user	5

Note: The percentage for non-users is higher than the 25 per cent in the survey who had never used any drugs because this includes those who had used drugs in the past but had since stopped using. Base n=200.

The ASMA classifications analysed by gender revealed no significant differences between the sexes and their degree of risk but there was when area location was taken into account. The majority of 'problematic' users (n=41) were found to be located in the South East of the country (n=23) compared to London (n=7), Merseyside (n=4) and the West Country (n=7). An analysis of the ASMA scores by age and ethnicity showed that the majority of 'problematic' users were aged between 17 and 19 years (n=30) and most were white (n=35). A further three were black, two were mixed race and one was Asian.

Correlations between drinking and drug use

In order to test whether regular or persistent patterns of drinking were correlated with problematic drug use, the ASMA drug risk scores were further compared with patterns of alcohol consumption, revealing a link between the two. Three-quarters of respondents who drank alcohol on three or more days of the week (n=19) were also identified as problematic drug users. Conversely, of those who were identified as problematic drug users (n=41), just one-third drank alcohol three to four, or more times a week. Most (41%) drank on an occasional basis or even less, suggesting that heavy drinkers were more likely to include drugs in their substance use intake, whereas this was not the case with heavy drug users. Indeed this verifies previous evidence that young people, aged 15 and 16 years who are 'heavy drinkers' are also more likely than others to smoke and to use illicit drugs (Plant *et al.*, 1985).

Drug use and problems correlated with family drug use

Just over a third of the sample (37%) had a family member who used drugs whilst they were growing up. A half (51%) said that no family members had used drugs to their knowledge. Of those who knew of a family member using drugs (n=74), most commonly it was their brother (15%), though 13 and ten per cent respectively were aware that their mother and/or father had previously, or were currently using drugs. In a minority of cases it was a sister (5%), a step parent or parent's partner (6%). The main reported familial choice of drug was cannabis, with 16 per cent saying a sibling smoked it, ten per cent saying their mother smoked it and eight per cent saying their father smoked it. At the more serious end of drug use, four per cent reported heroin was used by either their mother, father, or a sibling, and four per cent reported a family member used cocaine.

Twice as many young people who had a family member who took drugs whilst they were growing up were themselves a problematic drug user, as measured by ASMA, compared to those young people who had no family member who used drugs (31% versus 15%). Although the causes of problem drug use are complex this suggests a strong personal-familial drug use link, which is in line with the general finding that there are significant interactions between family environment and drug misuse (Advisory Council on the Misuse of Drugs, 1998; Pearson, 2000).

Changes in drug using patterns

Finally, the way in which drug use among these young people had changed over the last year was explored. As with alcohol consumption the overall trend was one of decline, though a fifth of the sample said they were using drugs more frequently than they had been.

Table 2.5: Respondents' drug use patterns over the last year

Drug using patterns over the last year	%
Never used any drugs	25
Stopped using drugs	22
Used drugs a bit less	7
Used drugs a lot less	11
Drug use stayed the same	16
Used drugs a bit more	7
Used drugs a lot more	12
Total	100

Note: Base=200.

Reasons given for these positive changes were due to:

- issues of finance
- accumulating more responsibility and maturing
- changing social groups
- feeling less need to experiment
- because of a personal (mental or physical) health scare
- witnessing friends and loved ones deteriorate as a consequence of prolonged drug misuse.

Of those respondents who claimed to be using drugs more frequently, the reasons cited for doing so were: because of peer group and social life changes; having more money; and increased availability of different drugs. Eleven indicated a self-medication style of drug use and one person said they were using more to combat loneliness.

To conclude, the trend over the 12 months before being interviewed was one in which the majority of the sample used fewer drugs or gave up altogether. This finding is consistent with similar research in the area (Measham *et al.*, 1998) that points to the transient nature of drug using patterns among youth populations, whereby inquisitive adolescents often grow out of an experimental phase in their lives.

In the following chapters evidence from the 30 follow-up interviews is reported. These explore what had occurred in young people's lives as they were leaving the care system or the parental home to live independently, and how drug use had interacted with this process of leaving and forging independent lives.

3   Changing patterns of drug use

The following section describes in detail the patterns of young people's drug use, what influenced their attitudes towards different drugs and therefore their use of certain drugs, and more specifically the way in which drug use was influenced by the process of leaving care to live independently. Where the self-report survey quantified the type and level of drug use among young care leavers, the in-depth interviews enabled a much fuller understanding of how drug use was bound up with this period of transition.

Given that the main focus of the study was to examine the way in which drug use developed and changed alongside the process of leaving care, it was necessary that the 30 young people selected for the in-depth interview had used drugs at some point in their lives. An alternative strategy would have been to include a sample of young people who had not used any drugs and explore whether they were initiated into them during this particular period of transition. For reasons of clarity the former approach was chosen and included young people who had used drugs in a fairly minor way and young people who had longer established patterns of drug use.

From this starting point the interviews with the sub-sample examined how drug use had altered over the course of their transition from care. The reasons for changing drug use are explored, for example whether they had begun to use drugs on a more frequent basis, or whether their drug using patterns had decreased, or remained the same and importantly what lay behind these changes.

The sample

The 30 young people selected to participate in the qualitative interview stage of the research reflected the wider sample, in terms of gender, age and ethnic background. The sample included young people who had lived within the care system as well as young people who had fled or left the family home at a young age with no social services' input. It was also important to include young people with different drug using experiences. For this reason some of the young people interviewed had extensive drug using histories and others had relatively short-lived minor experiences. The table below illustrates the main characteristics of the follow-up sample. One aspect in which the sample differed from the wider sample was that almost a third (n=9) had a child or at least one on the way, compared to a seventh (14%) in the wider sample. Whilst a few young people who were already parents were deliberately included in the follow-up sample, the increase in those who had become a parent or were soon to be between the first interview contact and the qualitative interview six months later, was a surprise.

Table 3.1: *Characteristics of the in-depth interview respondents*

Gender	Age range (& average)	Ethnic background		Area of country		Accommodation status	
Female 17	16 to 23	White	23	London	13	Own flat	12
Male 13	(18)	Black	3	Merseyside	3	Supported	
		Mixed race	4	West Country	4	lodgings	13
				South East	10	Other	5

Note: 'Other' accommodation types included imprisonment, living with foster, extended or partner's family. Base=30.

The leaving care process

In order to explore the way in which drug using patterns and careers were influenced by the process of leaving care, it was necessary to look at the types of transition from care these young people had been making and indeed were still making. From the interviews it was apparent they could be categorised into two types of leaver. These were those who had made a relatively smooth transition, and those who had experienced, or were still experiencing chaotic transitions to independence. Chaotic transitions were closely correlated with heavy drug use.

Smooth transitions to independence

Two key features identified smooth transitions. The first feature was when young people experienced relatively few changes in accommodation after leaving their last care placement (either foster families or children's homes). The second feature was when young people became settled in their own flats within a fairly short time period, or were soon to do so, either on their own or with a partner. Smooth transitions were assisted by a variety of factors. Despite growing up within complicated family relationships, some young people in the sample possessed high levels of resilience. Within the expanding research arena on young adulthood, there is a growing interest in how it is that some young people can cope better with the same set of circumstances than others. This area of study is still underdeveloped and to date has not provided any clear answers (Garmezy, 1996).

Chaotic transitions to independence

Chaotic transitions referred to those young people whose transition experience had been one in which their lives had fairly much fallen apart for a period of time, including periods of homelessness, drug problems, staying in numerous hostels, and forming inappropriate and exploitative relationships. These occurred for a range of reasons though at the point of interview most had come through this period of upheaval.

Some of the young people included in the sample were still in the process of making their way to full independence and were still living in supported accommodation. A number of those interviewed were still in transition, in what has been referred to as a "yo-yo" position, moving back and forwards between being looked after and supported and moving to independent living arrangements.

Changes in drug use patterns

To look at the ways drug use had changed from one period to the next it was necessary to examine what these young people's earlier patterns of drug use had been. It was necessary, as others who have attempted to define drug use during the adolescent and young adult years have done, to view drug use as a continuum over the course of this age and time period. Here the study drew on the work of Parker and colleagues (1998) who from their cohort study of adolescents in the north west of England referred to the 'in transition' state of adolescent drug users. They concluded that 'drug use across the adolescent years was part of a complex process of rational decision-making best viewed as a continuum of contrasting decisions with periods of abstinence and use throughout the late teenage years'. Applying this framework was useful to capture the fluctuating patterns of drug use that were found to be occurring among the sample of young adults in this study.

Briefly this part of the investigation captured drug use spanning the years from age 12/13 when some had at least begun smoking cannabis, through to the 17/18/19 age mark, which was the age most were when they participated in the in-depth interview. As revealed in the quantitative survey, the most common pattern of drug use across these years began with cannabis smoking around 14-years-old, progressing on to other drugs such as amphetamines and ecstasy and at its most extreme moving on to using heroin and crack cocaine. Where for most there was a sequential movement through these stages of drug experimentation, a few young people in the sample were very early drug users. Rather than moving through the stages sequentially, their drug use had peaked to a point of seriousness early in their drug using years.

In order to get a clearer view of the drug use among the sample a similar approach was adopted to that used by Measham *et al.*, (1998). In their study of the changing patterns of drug use among a group of adolescents, they developed a drug user typology. Based on the accounts of their drug use the young people in the qualitative study were divided in to three broad categories of drug user. These were:

- 'moderate occasional' drug users, which incorporated cannabis smoking and short-lived or controlled use of other drugs such as amphetamines, ecstasy and cocaine;

- 'regular poly' drug use referred to a sustained period of committed drug taking often associated with the dance/nightclub scene within which a whole range of drugs were consumed;

- 'problem' drug use referred to becoming addicted to heroin and/or crack cocaine, though also included drug use which could be defined as chaotic in the sense that other aspects of their lives had fallen into decline as a result, such as becoming homeless or becoming involved in crime to fund the cost of drugs.

If these young people's drug use is looked at as a fluctuating continuum, with periods of more and less use across the teenage years, at the point they participated in the in-depth interview it was apparent the majority had passed through their peak period of drug using. This had occurred, both earlier and later in the teenage years, and at the point of interview drug use was subsequently on the decline. It is of course possible this pattern could change and those who had since brought their drug use under control could revert to earlier patterns of more reckless drug using behaviour. However, the majority who discussed reducing their drug use or having stopped using drugs altogether, described this alongside having made significant life changes for the better.

Table 3.2 illustrates the changes in the in-depth interview sample's drug use across the teenage years. The nature of the drug-using peak varied by individual. Just a few had a maximum peak of moderate occasional use. The majority had gone beyond this, whereby for a time at least, their drug use had become entrenched mirroring the regular poly drug use described above. Over a third had stepped even further over the line to the point where their drug use had become problematic and as already noted for some this peak had been reached at the age of 13/14 revealing very early problem drug use.

Most of this sample had reached the peak of their drug taking around the age of 16/17, which coincided with the point at which most were experiencing increased levels of independence from their previous care arrangements. This was also the age point at which they were encouraged through social services to take on more responsibility in regards to their own care and livelihood. If the British Crime Survey is taken as a reliable indicator of the drug using patterns of the general population, it is apparent that this sample of young people's drug use had peaked at a much younger age. Year on year the British Crime Survey has recorded that the peak age of drug use occurs between the ages of 20 to 24 before tailing off (Ramsay and Spiller, 1997; Ramsay and Partridge, 1999; Ramsay *et al.*, 2001).

Table 3.2:   *Changes in drug use of the in-depth interview sample across the teenage years*

Maximum peak of drug use		Drug use at point of the in-depth interview		
Moderate occasional	x 7	Moderate occasional	x11	+4
Regular poly	x 11	Regular poly	x 5	-6
Problem	x 12	Problem	x 5	-7
		Abstainer	x 9	

Note: Base=30.

At the point when these young people were interviewed, drug use for most had levelled out to moderate occasional drug use or no drug use at all. A few could still be categorised as regular poly drug users. This was mostly linked with nightclub culture and/or socialising within tight-knit friendship groups where smoking cannabis was a common activity. Just five young people could be classed as problematic drug users at that point.

Whether those who were still taking drugs in a committed way at the point of interview, including regular poly and problematic users, were at the peak of their drug-using period was unknown. It seemed likely that this was the highest level the five regular poly drug users, whose drug use centred on the nightclub scene, would reach. Perhaps mirroring the rigorous health and safety campaigns surrounding drug use within the dance culture, these young people were well-informed about both the short and long-term health hazards surrounding ecstasy and were certainly bearing these messages in mind:

You have got to take responsibility every time you take an ecstasy tablet; you could be putting your life in danger.

Young people whose drug use centred around the dance club scene such as these tended to have strong opinions about what they considered to be the harder end drugs and indicated their drug use had a cut-off point:

The people that I do drugs with won't go near smack [heroin] or crack,… they have got the same kind of opinions as me.

Negative reactions, such as this, towards highly stigmatised drugs such as heroin and crack cocaine have been noted in other research on drug markets and among people who are otherwise committed to a drug using lifestyle (Parker, 2000; Pearson, 2001; Pearson and Hobbs, 2001). Whether these attitudes can be taken as reliable indicators that patterns of drug consumption among this care leaver sample will remain relatively stable or continue their downward path is a crucial question.

Attitudes towards different drugs shaping drug use

The extent to which this sample of young people had become involved in drug use, still used drugs, or had stopped using certain or all drugs was based on their experiences of different drugs and their observation of other people's use, notably others demise through heavy drug use.

In line with the responses revealed in the survey, the majority of the follow-up sample viewed cannabis smoking to be relatively harmless and barely worth mentioning within a discussion of drugs. For example, one young woman's drug use had only ever included smoking cannabis and taking ecstasy, and in the interview she stated emphatically that she did not even consider herself a drug user:

I don't take drugs, I don't class myself as a drug taker, I smoke weed and I'll take an 'e' [ecstasy tablet] *to have a good time in a club.*

This *laissez-faire* attitude towards cannabis was based on the widely felt notion that *'it was everywhere'*, and *'everybody was on it'*, and here they were not only referring to young people. It was viewed that the pervasiveness of cannabis across society, though especially among their peers, meant along the way they had naturally encountered it, and once they had begun smoking it, they had simply continued. Most believed smoking cannabis did not affect their health, though it was apparent these judgments came from the more moderate smokers. Those who had been or were still heavy cannabis smokers acknowledged the negative impact on motivation, especially. One young man who smoked cannabis heavily and had no plans to cut down, admitted that it did make him *'lazy'*. The negative impact on functioning from cannabis smoking and other drugs was presented as a concern in an interview with a foyer project manager. He found that young people's preparedness to experiment with drugs in a relatively casual manner meant that they were neglecting other important things in their lives, and that this could hinder their progress and development:

> I think most of them would say "we would never take heroin" …but there are other drugs in pill format that I think they are quite happy to experiment with and then find it difficult to concentrate on the other things in life i.e. jobs or training, so I certainly think there is a link there that impinges on their ability to move on.

On the whole, ecstasy, amphetamines and cocaine were treated with more caution by these young people though, as already noted, some in this group had virtually relegated ecstasy to the status of a 'harmless' drug. This view was perhaps encouraged by the fact that ecstasy on the whole was used within nightclub settings and on a relatively infrequent basis, mainly on the weekends. A few acknowledged that they had underestimated the impact that drugs like ecstasy and cocaine could have on their general health and well being. One young man, whose use of ecstasy, ketamine and cocaine was compounded by the fact that he worked in a nightclub said:

> It was stopping me from functioning properly during the daytime because I was either asleep or ill from the come down [after effects] of the drugs.

Across the board young people separated crack and heroin out from other drugs, placing them in a league of their own and making it clear that their drug use stopped at that point:

> I do coke [cocaine], but I don't do anything heavier than that.

Along the way though a few had been trapped in a phase of serious substance abuse in which heroin, alongside a host of other drugs, had been a feature. Here, rather than separating out specific drugs as being a primary culprit in the chaotic drug experience, a whole gamut of drugs and the particular life period were viewed as the problem. Of those who had developed chaotic drug using lifestyles, there was a distinct tendency for them also to have experienced both emotional and physical abuse in their earlier lives, serious family dysfunction and an inability to cope with early independence.

An interesting dimension observed within this style of drug use was, of the range of drugs taken to block out their painful feelings, heroin was still often stigmatised and most said they would never consider using it. In response to being asked his opinions on heroin, one young man, who was using a range of drugs at the point of interview and in applying the typology was categorised as a problematic drug user, said:

I just don't want to do that sort of thing, loads of my mates have been really addicted to it and I don't want to end up becoming addicted to it as well because it just f***s up your life, heroin does and I don't want that to happen to me.

Interestingly, one young man defended his occasional use of heroin and crack cocaine within notions of it not being possible to become addicted if use was kept at a low level of frequency:

The only way you can get addicted to it is if you do it everyday, but if you're just doing it like once every two or three months, then that's not going to do you any damage in the long run then, is it?

This type of justification for personal styles of drug use has been framed well by Shiner and Newburn (1997). They applied the concept of neutralisation techniques to the tactic young people used to rationalise the types of drug use in which they were engaged. In effect, that is what this young man was doing. His conveniently held misguided health information surrounding heroin and crack cocaine enabled him to continue using them in the same way as he had been:

I'm not going to buy any gear [heroin] *or crack or any coke* [cocaine], *if somebody wants to offer me some, then I'll smoke it.*

Addiction was the point of reference that many of these young people used in defending the extent to which they used drugs, justifying their continuing use on the grounds that they were *'not addicted'*.

Reasons behind increases in drug using patterns

There are numerous individual reasons why someone's pattern of drug use might increase. Here, just two that emerged from the in-depth interviews are discussed, since they both have a bearing on how young care leavers' transitions to independent living are planned and managed. The first is the use of hostels as half-way houses and the nature of the 'hostel culture' that can sometimes involve tight-knit drug using peer subcultures. The second is when young people's experiences of leaving care are premature or poorly planned, resulting in fragile living situations with which some care leavers are unable to cope.

Hostel culture

Where the association between drug use and other life factors is complex, there was a significant correlation with increased levels of drug use and moving from the care system or the family home to live independently. One aspect where this was most apparent was with the type of culture that grew up in the hostel accommodation many of these young people found themselves living in while waiting to be allocated a more permanent roof over their heads. This covered foyer projects as well as the more traditional homeless hostels. Here young people reported the main change to their drug use was a progression on from cannabis to other drugs like ecstasy and cocaine, and a tendency to use them on a much more frequent basis than they had previously been accustomed.

Drug use within the hostel environment was described within the context of typical teenage socialising, peer association and going out as a group to nightclubs. On exploring how the drug using habits of others rubbed off on their own, a young woman provided the following explanation:

> If your peer group are experimenting then you think it is only natural and you'll do it and that is what I thought and that's why I started doing more, because everybody else was doing it and it was the thing to do.

Similarly, another young woman alluded to the camaraderie that existed around the socialising and drug use that was going on within the hostel where she was living as providing a 'family feeling'. As well as the hostel environment sometimes being viewed as fun and supportive, young people also noted that being accommodated with a number of similar aged young people could encourage an unproductive atmosphere and group behaviour in which heavy drug use and drinking became the norm. Descriptions were provided of gathering in each others bedrooms, where day and night merged into one, and reckless quantities of drink and drugs were consumed. Another young man, who described falling into a pattern of heavy drug use within the hostel where he lived, deliberately moved himself out, to curtail the heavy pattern of drinking and drug use he had become involved in:

> I got a bit too full on with the drinking and I had enough of that, and living there wasn't doing me any good so I phoned my sister and said look can I take you up on your offer of moving in with you ...I said 'cause my drinking has become too much.

It must be added that in moving himself out, this young man jeopardised his position of housing need and at the time of the interview continued to live with his sister, her husband and their two children.

Although young people noted how the hostel dynamic fuelled this style of drug use, they also acknowledged it was as much to do with their own willingness to experiment with drugs at a somewhat higher level. However, it was apparent that not becoming involved required a strong character and a secure identity around their own drug using decisions. Neither appeared easy. Young people expressed the transition from care to independent living as being unsettling and stressful.

Being part of a group, whatever the activity, appealed and served a useful purpose at that particular stage of the transition. Hagan and McCarthy (1998) in a North American study of youth crime and homelessness refer to what they term 'street families' which while they can accelerate someone's involvement in deviant behaviour, also serve a positive function of friendship and support. The young woman's comment of the 'family feeling' of being in a hostel culture has already been noted.

The ability to resist drugs, especially drugs that were not viewed as exceptionally harmful, such as cannabis and ecstasy, was a skill not usually acquired until after someone had passed through their own phase of experimentation. One young woman had made her mind up about drugs at a quite early age. Having been drawn into a street drug culture and subsequent addiction, she had stopped using them. So that although she was living in a hostel with others who were 'hard-end' drug users, who on occasion attempted to encourage her to join them in their drug use, this was not something she was prepared to be drawn into:

> Now I have done it [given up taking drugs], I have not started again for about three months.

Premature departure from care and not coping

How some young people began forging their independence whilst still accommodated within the care system is mentioned above. It was evident that a few young people within our sample had been moved on from care, or been driven from the parental home, prematurely. This was a situation that some found they were unable to cope with and to varying degrees, drinking and drug use had become a crutch. Another young woman's initiation into serious drug use was unarguably related to the leaving care process. She had felt unable to cope with what she considered a premature departure from care, and the feelings of desperation and loneliness that had set in while living in a flat on her own with little support from social services:

They just put me there and I didn't know what to do and I walked out, just gave up.

Similarly, on reaching the official age at which young people are moved from care to live independently, a young man alluded to the abrupt nature of the move and said he had felt *'slung out'*. His case was bound by the earlier childcare legislation that allowed local authorities to move young people from care to live independently at the age of 16. He was moved into a YMCA hostel and had lived there ever since. He was 23 at the point of interview and revealed a propensity to drink from earlier in his teen years. He openly discussed his family's history of alcohol misuse and connected his ongoing pattern of heavy drinking to a feeling of abandonment on being moved from care and his frustration and depression with not having managed to move on ever since:

> *It's like when I think of personal things, my situation and everything like that, it tends to make me drink.*

These young people did not often make the association between their drug and/or alcohol consumption and the premature independence they were experiencing. However, it was apparent the stresses they described were a feature of the circumstances they had encountered while attempting to cope on their own and were a contributory factor to the sometimes damaging patterns of drug and alcohol consumption they went on to develop. This was particularly apparent for the five young people in the sample who had left the family home to live alone, at a young age. Despite qualifying for social services support and assistance, all of these young people had struggled along relying on their own resources, and what support they could glean from others along the way.

Fed up with the alcohol-related violence going on within her family home, another young woman *'walked out'* at the age of 14. After an unhappy, brief spell in a social services run children's home she left there to go it alone. Here she described a period of three years when she was in a series of volatile boyfriend relationships, living in a host of emergency night shelters and hostels, abusing drugs and alcohol before hitting rock bottom, whereupon social services became involved:

> *I hit the drink really hard and heavy and it just, it sorted me out, at the time I thought it sorted me out but it just made me worse and er... it was just hard being on my own, being young, it's hard fending for yourself.*

Reasons behind decreases in drug using patterns

As well as seeing increases in the extent to which drugs were being used alongside the process of leaving care, a majority of young people interviewed had reduced their drug use. As Table 3.1 illustrated, overall the pattern within the sample was of decreasing use, stabilisation, or quitting the use of drugs. The most common shifts were from regular poly drug use to moderate occasional use, together with a shift from problem drug use to not using any drugs at all. In line with the survey findings, a few noted that in cutting down on their drug consumption their alcohol intake had increased.

Maturity and increased responsibilities

In general, these patterns of decreased drug use were seen by young people to reflect a growing sense of maturity and increased responsibilities. In the drugs research literature, the process of 'maturing out' is commonly found to be something associated with older age cohorts. Also it is commonly provoked by an important relationship change or other significant life event, together with behaviour changes resulting from direct experiences of the damaging effects of prolonged drug misuse (Biernacki, 1986; Waldorf et al., 1991). Here, there appear to be similar experiences in much younger age groups.

For example, another young man expressed the view that he had simply grown out of his earlier cavalier lifestyle of drinking and drug taking – 'just don't need to do it all the time'. Although he was also looking forward to soon acquiring the status of fatherhood, which was playing a big part in his altered views on drug use and his patterns of consumption, his thoughts were also framed within a general air of maturing and looking to a healthier future. He remembered fairly recently when he used to smoke cannabis 'all day' and couldn't understand how some of his contemporaries remained at that stage, such as the young man who used to share his supported lodgings. He continued to see his friend every now and again and remarked, 'once he stops smoking he will realise ... he will be a better person'.

Another important factor was the practical, day-to-day responsibilities of independent living. Young people in the sub-sample were at different points in the process of becoming independent. Some were already residing in their own flats and were living with the responsibility of running a household. For those who had not yet reached this point, the move was imminent. Indeed, a few were delaying the move from supported living arrangements simply because they felt they weren't yet ready to do so. For those who had already moved and those who were soon to, the responsibilities of running a flat and managing a household budget were only too real and demanding. Unhindered drug use alongside these weighty responsibilities was considered incompatible.

Another way of expressing these transitions to independent living was that, having acquired a feeling of stability on getting their own place, the young people concerned were not about to jeopardise this by letting their drug use get out of hand. One young woman had previously lost her flat and became homeless when her heroin addiction had got out of hand. This time she was determined not to repeat the same mistakes:

> I've been waiting a long time and where I went wrong the first time I ain't going wrong again.

Becoming a parent

The relatively high proportion of the sub-sample who were parents, or who would do so soon, has already been noted. Parenthood and pregnancy had a definite impact on the way these young people viewed not only their drug use, but their more general responsibilities. Overall, cannabis smoking was felt to be acceptable and to have little impact on parenting. Indeed, most continued to smoke and the women in particular reported that it helped them cope with the added stresses of having a baby. Other drug use though was considered much more serious and unacceptable.

The six young women in the in-depth interview sample who were parents voiced more concern about drug use and parenthood than the three men who were parents. For the girls, the threat of having their child taken away from them by social services was very real. Four of the six had been drug addicted in the recent past and although they were determined to remain drug free, most were still vulnerable to relapse. Two young women had already experienced the trauma of having their babies taken into care, albeit temporarily, and even those who had not were living with a great deal of pressure to prove themselves. A young woman, who experienced a stressful period alongside the birth of her baby, had a brief spell of returning to smoking crack cocaine. Rationalising the consequences, if she was to continue, helped her to quit:

> I put an ultimatum on my head if I continued using the drugs, what's going to happen? I am either going to keep my daughter or I am going to lose my daughter, basically I am going to lose my daughter if I continue taking drugs ...so I thought right what's the best way, I want to keep my daughter.

Where pregnancy and parenthood assisted for the most part to curtail drug use, the removal of a child into care also prompted the use of more drugs or drink:

That was really bad, I hit the drink. I hit the drink really bad, I was drunk all the time, it was really bad, it tore me up, it tore me up big time, I was stressed out, I didn't eat anything, I was just drinking all the time, drugs, I was just doing a lot of stuff that I just really shouldn't have been doing.

Addiction and health consequences

A more common reason for young people's reduced levels of drug use was the negative health consequences they had begun to experience, or seen in others. It has already been noted that some young people in the sample had experienced drug addiction. Apart from two of these, all had overcome this at the point of interview. However, it is fair to add that given this was a recent experience and because many of these young people's lives continued to involve high levels of instability and stress, a return to 'risky' drug use was a potential hazard.

A few young people using drugs such as ecstasy, 'speed' and cocaine had reached levels of use that resulted in health problems. This was despite not becoming addicted, and being able to curtail their use:

I am still recovering from ecstasy and that's a long time ago since I've taken ecstasy.

Some young people had been able to cope with the spell of heavy drug use they were drawn into with friends, or within hostel accommodation, either by imposing their own controls and *'cutting down'*, or even moving out of the hostel. It was evident some were not so able. The drug using group which one young man had associated had split up, mainly because those he had been involved with had moved out from the supported lodgings. However, he was still feeling the repercussions of his former drug using. Along with his friends, he had fallen into a pattern of regular nightclub going and taking the range of drugs associated with this particular lifestyle such as ecstasy, LSD and cocaine. Although he had enjoyed his drug use at the time, it had left scars on him and when interviewed he was still overcoming its impact on both his physical and mental functioning.

Young man: *I felt, kind of, really low before, even weak minded.*

Interviewer: *When you say 'before', how long ago are you talking about?*

Young man: *Last year... and the year before that and basically I just felt weak. You know in that I didn't feel strong like, I couldn't even be bothered to get out of bed but at that time that was kind of normal, you know. It's easier looking back now and saying this but at the time you just kind of keep going.*

A couple of young people were still in the midst of this style of drug using and had no plans to alter their weekend use, but they were in a minority. Most of the young people in the sub-sample had managed to withdraw from potentially damaging levels of drug misuse. This was as a result of their growing sense of maturity, new responsibilities that were incompatible with persistent drug misuse, or a more positive attitude towards their personal health, which would often have reflected a growing sense of self-esteem.

4   Support and service provisions for care leavers

All those who took part in the in-depth interviews had some form of drug using experience, whether it was problematic or not. This chapter explores the types of support and service provision young people in the study who had been, or were currently experiencing drug use problems, drew upon; the extent to which they utilised such services; and which services or approaches were found to be most appropriate to their needs. The relationship between degrees of coping and ability to seek help are also explored. Interwoven within this chapter is evidence drawn from interviews carried out with leaving care team staff and other agency personnel on how they perceived young people's help-seeking in relation to drug use and the specific role they played in the process.

Two main avenues of support were accessed. These could be broadly grouped into *formal* and *informal* sources of help. Each is described in turn below. The types and levels of support these young people sought and relied upon varied depending upon what provisions were available to them. Indeed, most used both formal and informal types of help intermittently.

Types of formal support

Social services

In England, on exiting the state care system every young person is entitled to assistance from a leaving care team. Although variously organised these are based in local authority social services departments. The organisation of after care support varies across local authorities as teams have discretion over localised resources and the division of services. However, as noted in the introduction, legislative changes laid out in the Children (Leaving Care) Act 2000 have placed a duty on social services departments to provide continued support and assistance to young care leavers up to the age of 18. This is to assist the transition to independence.

The way in which leaving care teams most commonly assisted young people in the study was by providing support with day-to-day practical living issues as they moved to independent living. This included practical help with accessing leaving care grants and other forms of financial support, securing accommodation, furnishing and decorating a new residence or assisting with budgeting and form filling tasks. On a more personal level, staff assisted by being available with a listening ear, offering advice in the role of a corporate parent or even liaising with the young person's family to encourage maintaining contact.

In relation to drug use, staff reported having casual conversations with young people on the need for caution surrounding their drug taking. In regard to problem drug use, involving drugs such as heroin and/or crack cocaine and addiction issues, leaving care team staff reported playing a referral role to more specialist agencies in that they would seek out available treatment options and make the necessary arrangements for entry to these facilities. It was apparent though that the referral process could be hindered by a lack of appropriate treatment options for this age group. On describing trying to access help for one young man who had become addicted to heroin, a leaving care team manager commented:

> There didn't seem to be much available and [for] what was available [there] was a waiting list. There was no immediate access.

Foyer projects

Foyer projects are an expanding service available to disadvantaged young people across the country. A small proportion of those who participated in the in-depth interview were housed in foyer project accommodation. Entry to this type of service is conditional on a young person's suitability in terms of their general stability and motivation to reach their potential and there is a strict policy of no illegal drugs allowed on the premises. The assessment is made in the form of an entrance interview, which was criticised by one member of staff in our study for excluding vulnerable young people from more chaotic backgrounds, in favour of prioritising places for more stable young people. This occurs primarily because foyer projects do not view themselves as equipped to deal with the sharp end of health problems that may be experienced by more vulnerable young people, such as mental ill-health or problem drug use. Indeed, it was found in the study that young people with more problematic drug using lifestyles were more likely to be living in and accessing services from (temporary) homeless hostels, such as night shelters and inner-city agencies targeting homeless young people.

Specialist drugs and alcohol services

Most of the harder end drug users in the sub-sample had experienced or were still experiencing health problems often related to their drug use. Both short-term and/or longer-term professional help had been accessed for such problems. This was either in the form of a young person being referred by social services or leaving care teams, or on a self-referral basis. The types of services drawn upon for assistance with drugs problems included the medical professions, such as local GPs, Accident and Emergency centres and specialist practitioners such as counsellors and psychiatrists from drugs and alcohol units offering detoxification and rehabilitation programmes. The following section covers young people's experiences of accessing these services.

Experiences of accessing and using formal support

Before receiving help for a drug problem from a formal support agency, it is necessary for a person to acknowledge and accept a problem exists and that they are in need of assistance. If an individual fails to acknowledge a problem, it is extremely difficult, if not impossible to help them. Indeed, this denial type behaviour surrounding 'risky' drug use was said to be a problem with a few young people in the study and made the work of those employed to assist them difficult. The following comment made by a leaving care team manager, expresses the way this could complicate their work:

> It's much easier to deal with that [someone who admits a problem], *than it is when you have got worries. You express those to young people and they deny it,* [drug use], *you are just stuck. They know you know they have got a problem, they still think they can handle it and it will come up in* [that] *they are desperate for money.*

As can be expected, individuals vary in their willingness to admit a problem and further differ in their ability to ask for help and knowing where to seek it. One young woman in this study was an example of someone who took some time to ask for help. She had left home prematurely following a family feud and subsequently ran away to London. Soon after she arrived in the capital, she found herself immersed in London's street culture and not long after became addicted to crack cocaine. For some time she failed to receive any help with her drugs problem simply because she did not know where to turn:

> *Basically when I came to London I didn't have anyone there for me, I didn't know what to do. I didn't know how to act, I didn't even know how to ask for help.*

Positive experiences of formal support

It is well known that drugs misuse is a feature of homeless and street-based lifestyles and many agencies, who specialise in working with 'the homeless', address drugs as a part of their working routine. Becoming a part of London's street culture eventually led this young woman to being pointed in the direction of an inner-city agency aimed at young homeless people. On presenting to the agency and admitting the problems that she was experiencing, the agency was able to assist her. Support over the longer-term was negotiated and by allocating her a multiple-needs worker, the other problems she was experiencing could also be addressed.

From her viewpoint, this form of help had helped her to build up resilience against relapse and to retain custody of her three-month old baby. She described the support and assistance received from the agency as being *'a tower of strength to me'*. In turn she described helping fellow hostel residents who were experiencing similar drug problems to those she had experienced:

I tell them how I got off it [crack cocaine] *and that basically gives them encouragement.*

Indeed, mutual peer assistance was found to be an important source of help to a number of the young people interviewed, and her experience illustrated how formal and informal support systems intersect. It was through her involvement in London's street culture that she first 'learned the ropes' of how to access appropriate formal help, and subsequently, she tried to pass on what she had learned to friends experiencing similar difficulties.

Clearly, an important factor for this young woman's success was the holistic approach adopted by the agency staff. This involved working with young people in addressing all aspects of their lives, rather than simply focusing on drug use issues in isolation from other problems such as housing, health, employment, finance, family relations and so on. The holistic model is beginning to be more widely used by a range of support services that work with young vulnerable people. A move towards incorporating a comprehensive needs assessment and viewing drug use as a symptom, not a cause, is a trend for many agencies, but is not yet as fully developed as it could be (SCODA, 1997; Health Advisory Service, 2001). As one leaving care team manager commented:

There has been a very big gap for a very long time but now it's getting better.

A close relationship between young people and staff working in formal support agencies was essential, in order to recognise when there was a need for help and to deliver the appropriate interventions. A good and consistent relationship was particularly important in cases where young people were engaging in illegal activities, such as using drugs like heroin and/or crack cocaine and committing crime or prostitution to fund their addiction. Young people need to feel confident and secure in revealing sensitive information, especially when information is open to judgement and they may risk prosecution. Some staff, including a manager of a housing provider for vulnerable young people described a working format, which appeared to set young people at ease when discussing sensitive issues:

As soon as they arrive we get them to identify the sorts of things that they need support with. Generally at the point of applying they put down very little. I guess they want to sell themselves positively and they want to make a good impression, so they tend to put down that they generally need very little support, except for things like filling in official forms, maybe to help identify where the nearest doctors and dentists are. So the sorts of things they are unlikely to be judged on. But what we find, very soon after they move in and feel relatively safe, is the whole list of things that we might offer in support which suddenly come to the fore.

Negative experiences of formal support

Not all the young people in the sample who could have benefited from formal support were found to be accessing agencies or services to receive the assistance they required. Young people were found to resist seeking and accepting formal help for a variety of reasons. For instance, some seemed to have become disillusioned with social services through their dealings with them over time, and as a consequence had developed a general distrust of formal agencies.

Those who held negative views about formal agencies tended to have experienced long and complicated care histories where formal agencies had played a significant role in their growing up. For example, frustrations around the practical difficulties of contacting social services staff *'they change every week'*, and *'they just haven't got the staff'* were common. This issue was indeed confirmed in staff interviews whereby similar complaints of high levels of staff turnover were made, emphasising the difficulty such shortages caused to their workloads.

It can be difficult, however, even for the most effective formal agency teams to intervene in the lives of young people who are engaging in serious drug use and living chaotic lifestyles. Here priorities can become confused whereby the importance of maintaining a relationship with support workers along with keeping their lives in order may be of low priority. One staff interviewee made the point:

Crack use is very familiar to us, you obviously work very hard to stop people getting involved in it but once people do become involved they become much less focused on the housing issues and obviously it affects their whole presentation and their motivation.

Keeping track of serious drug users

The more serious drug users in the sub-sample, such as those using heroin or crack cocaine, had different priorities and motivations towards seeking help compared to those who did not use these drugs. The research showed how difficult it could be to track down young people falling into this category, presumably because of the chaotic lifestyles they were leading. Indeed, there were five individuals targeted from the original sample for in-depth interviews where the second contact failed. Each was known to be using either heroin and/or crack cocaine at the time. This was symptomatic of the problem, and in such cases effective help is likely to be a challenge.

Gaps in provision of formal support

There is, however, a very real shortage of provision for young people, whether in the form of drug treatment or more general mental health services. A study conducted by Lewis (2000) on behalf of the National Children's Bureau, found that few suitable psychiatric and psychological provisions existed for young people aged 16 to 18 years with acknowledged or diagnosed mental health problems. Lewis argued that this group were neither considered to be children nor adults: too old for the children and family services, but too young for the adult services (Ashton, 1999). This gap in services was indeed a recurrent theme throughout the interviews carried out with staff. A practising senior social worker from the south east of England area stated:

> Between 15 and 16 and even 16-and-a-half we just have no [mental health] services for those young people. It's just not there, you know maybe people are putting themselves up to say yes: "we do deliver a service to those young people". But it doesn't happen.

Similarly, on the issue of artificial divisions between youth and adult services and there being a general lack of suitable provision, one staff manager drew the following parallel:

> Adult services kick in at 18 which aren't appropriate for our young people. ... It's a bit like the criminal justice system, at 18 you are into an adult system and it doesn't fit.

The finding that not all young people in the study who were suffering from (mental) health and/or drugs problems were receiving appropriate professional interventions was further evidence of the system's neglect of this vulnerable section of society. Even where services are available there is a long recognised difficulty of effective communication, particularly where counselling and behavioural interventions are concerned. Making professional interventions relevant and meaningful to the recipients of services is a challenge (Mayer and Timms, 1970). One young man in the study described how he had stopped seeing the psychiatrist to whom he had been referred because he could not see the point of it:

He just used to ask me, how I am doing and that. And just like, what kind of day I have had. ... Just talk about the same old stuff really.

Finding and accessing informal support

In line with the general population, many of the young people in the sample said they often tapped into informal networks of support. These included asking for help and accepting assistance from friends, family, partners, partners' family members or in some cases, previous foster family members. Participants approached and received help from different people depending on their unique set of background circumstances. Those individuals with particularly long and more chaotic care histories and severed family ties were unable to draw on informal networks. The discussion here focuses upon the young people's reasons for using and experiences of these informal networks.

Individuals varied considerably in terms of whom they informally approached and received help from. All participants had either experienced some period in institutional care, or run away from the family home at a young age. Consequently, in all cases, family relations were estranged to some degree at some point in these young people's lives. The frequency and quality of reunited relationships varied. A few did not know their parents or at least their parent's whereabouts at the point of interview. In other cases however, the young person maintained some form of contact with their families, but they were unable to rely on them as a means of support. Others seemed to rely heavily on re-united family relationships with members or familial substitutes and/or friends and partners. They found this to be more relevant than the formal sources of support available to them.

Young people's reasons for seeking informal support were just as wide ranging as to those they turned. Sometimes it was for financial and practical assistance, but more often than not it was for emotional support. Informal sources served multifunctional roles. They provided a sense of belonging, security, identity, encouragement, a listening ear, or personal advice and guidance and so on. Different individuals were approached to suit individual needs.

Positive experiences of informal support

In seeking assistance with drug use issues in particular, many of the young people reported turning to friends, partners, extended biological and ex-foster family members for help. This was especially the case when immediate family relationships were strained, if not severed, and formal help was not a viable option. Many of the young people, particularly those from more problematic family backgrounds, were typically mutually supportive of each other. For example, one young woman, whose serious drug problems were mentioned in the previous chapter, pointed to her boyfriend and friends as the main positive influence in helping her to give up drugs:

> The only reason I stopped was because he [partner] asked me to. If it weren't for him I'd still be doing it now. I'd probably be in a right state. … It was either carry on with drugs or lose my friends and they were the only real sort of people I felt I could trust.

In this case, her peers helped in many ways, for example, by being positive role models in that they were 'not into the drug scene' themselves and hence employed shock tactics in an attempt to change her drug using behaviours:

> They used to sort of have a go if they caught me doing it because they would both [partner and best friend] read up on what aerosols did and they told me I was going to end up with holes in my brain.

She also received help from a drugs, alcohol and abuse centre that employed a range of different strategies.

Being in a loving relationship with a partner was found to be a stabilising feature in a number of these young people's lives. More often than not young people's drug taking behaviour was influenced positively by their partners who generally assisted them in their transition to adulthood. This was found to be especially true for male interviewees, where girlfriends seemed to offer a strong sense of support. This was clearly demonstrated by a young man who, when describing his process of giving up previous heavy use of cannabis, ecstasy, amphetamines and cocaine, said:

> All you need is a good Mrs to give you a good kick up the backside.

For these individuals it seemed that accepting the responsibilities of being in a relationship changed their lifestyle choices. A romantic partner generally had a positive influence in assisting the young person to keep on track. Partners and friends were often pillars of strength and were frequently cited as mainstay figures in their lives.

Negative experiences of informal support

Sadly, this was not always the case. In the study it appeared that a few young women had experienced destructive and exploitative relationships, when ex-partners had influenced their drug and alcohol use in negative ways. One such case was a young woman who believed:

> If I wasn't with him I wouldn't have done the types of drugs that I have done.

She left her drug dealing boyfriend by escaping to a women's refuge prior to moving to a foyer project. Mainly through her own strength, she also managed to overcome her addiction to cocaine and crack cocaine and had stopped her heavy drinking. Indeed, most of the young people interviewed who were escaping similarly problematic relationships drew on their own resilience in overcoming their drug problems. They usually said they had learnt through experience:

> I am older now, I know what to do, I know who to invite and who not to invite. It's good, 'cause I am away from all of this [drug using peers from homelessness agency].

Parents/premature leaving home

In cases where parental direction had been minimal, if not non-existent, a young person had little choice but to be resilient. For example, one young man having recently come through the worst of his drug use reflected:

> It's like some parental guidance would be good but it's not to be. It's just down to myself I suppose.

A few young people in the sub-sample experienced a role reversal while they had been growing up. They had provided support and looked after their parents with alcohol and drugs problems. One such example was the case of a young woman who was taken into care at the age of 12 due to her mother's heroin and crack cocaine addiction and consequent involvement in prostitution. Witnessing the negative effects of drug use had the positive effect of discouraging her from using heroin or crack cocaine herself:

> I have seen what my Mum has done. My Mum has lost everything, everything. Everything. She hasn't even got a house. She sleeps in other people's houses now.

In other cases, however, a few young people reported leaving home when their own involvement in drug use led to parental disapproval or inability to cope:

> *Basically I wanted my independence. I wanted to do what I wanted to do, not what she* [mother] *wanted.*

At the point where their drug problems became out of control, these young people would be more likely to turn to other sources of support outside the family unit. Often this included informally turning to substitute carers, such as partners' families or in some cases ex-foster families. It is at this stage in the young person's drug using career where young care leavers or runaways can be seen to be most vulnerable.

The central importance of the natural family in coping with drug crises can be judged by the upsurge of parents' groups following the onset of the heroin epidemic in the 1980s (Donoghoe *et al.*, 1987; Dorn *et al.*, 1987; Pearson *et al.*, 1985). For care leavers, this vital source of support is invariably not an option. Vulnerability is increased if few informal options are available to them and they are unaware of what formal support is on offer or there are difficulties in accessing and trusting formal avenues of help.

For the fortunate, informal sources of support were often described very positively by the young people in the sub-sample. Their role of intervening and supporting was generally regarded to be of help in many ways. They provided positive role models by disapproving and disciplining drug use and many of the young people responded well to this input. Some foster parents even went so far as to having been directly involved with the detoxification process when the young person was trying to withdraw from drugs. Many carers, friends and partners were seen to take a very hands-on role in assisting young people with drug issues and were a greatly valued source of support.

5   Discussion and conclusion

It was clear from this study that for a variety of reasons young care leavers were vulnerable with respect to drug use and misuse. This was related to various factors: adverse childhood experiences, the feelings of loss and fragmentation that often characterise the experience of living in care, normal teenage peer association, and being faced with difficult challenges and responsibilities on leaving the care system. However, it should be stressed that for the majority drug use was a passing phase that began to decline alongside incurring adult responsibilities.

Clearly, there were young people who used drugs as part of the adolescent progression towards adulthood, whose drug use presented them with few problems and whose use was barely distinguishable from other teenagers in the general population. There were others who had run into problems with drugs at a young age, although as other areas of their lives had begun to stabilise, for instance finding more permanent accommodation or rekindling family relationships, seemed to have been overcome. A minority, who had developed persistent and worrying patterns of substance misuse, would need the support and assistance of specialist services and professionals for some time to come.

Drugs education

This study pointed to opportunities for drugs education with young care leavers. While it might seem an anomaly to talk about providing drugs education to a group of young people whose drug use was well established, some opportunities were revealed where specific type of drugs education would be beneficial. The opportunities were education focusing on helping young people to resist the pressure to use drugs or to resist progressing on to other forms of drug use. A member of staff from a central London agency for 'the homeless' described one of the early and important warning messages that they gave to young people who turned up at their service. This was to stress that alongside their homelessness and street living they were likely to encounter hard drugs, such as crack cocaine and heroin, and as well people who were keen to get them involved in using these drugs.

These same kind of resistance warnings or encouragement ought to be given to young people on entry into the more independent natured group living arrangements, such as foyer projects and young people centred hostels. One problem identified with these accommodation types was that they had frequently adopted a 'zero tolerance' policy to drugs, in such a way as to preclude the possibility that such simple drugs prevention messages were passed on. Where young people had become involved in drug use in a range of ways, a number of them found their willpower was severely challenged by the peer-group dynamic within hostels and foyer projects so that they had become drawn into more harmful forms of drinking and drug taking. In such circumstances, 'zero tolerance' actually meant wilful neglect.

As a result of this finding a more realistic policy is recommended which addresses drug use rather than ignoring it in these types of living arrangements. A young person's induction into a hostel or foyer project placement should include a pep talk from staff to forewarn them. The talk should stress that drugs are an issue and that they might well encounter situations where they feel pressured by others to consume drugs and that the option of resisting is a reasonable one.

Leaving and after care team support

All of the young people interviewed had accessed some form of support in relation to their drug using and/or more general life problems at some point in their move towards independence. The main avenue of support available to young care leavers with estranged family backgrounds was to access members of staff from leaving and after care teams. The results of this study revealed that after care support workers in the majority of cases had a direct influence and positive impact on these young people's lives. Whilst this was true for the majority, it was apparent some leaving and after care services were poorly managed and under resourced. As a result, the needs of the young people they were supposed to be serving were going unmet.

Given that many of these young people were without any family support and were indeed young, this was a depressing situation. Although steps were being taken to improve the shortage of personnel across the social care profession, there is an urgent need for a sense of value to be restored to the profession. Social services departments need to be able to attract and recruit the highly skilled and competent people to work with vulnerable populations, such as these young people.

Setting this broader social care problem aside social services are the lead agency in assisting young care leavers with transition issues, including drug problems. Staff, therefore, need to be adequately prepared to respond to drug-related issues. In order for members of staff to be successful in their interactions with young people in regard to this, a number of issues became apparent. Firstly, the young people need to admit that they are facing difficulties relating to drug use. A person in denial of a problem was not a likely candidate for intervention or treatment of any kind. Secondly, to encourage a young person's motivation for seeking help, staff must be available, approachable, knowledgeable and perceptive. The building of a positive and trusting relationship between young people and staff members was found to be of crucial importance in assisting smooth transitions to independence.

While staff of leaving care teams were effective in their relationships with young people, it is imperative that the basic social work training and other training is in place for those who work with young people. Training needs to be enhanced to include a comprehensive understanding of the complexities surrounding drug use and treatment issues.

Young runaways

It has been noted that young people who run away from home at an early age often do not come into contact with any form of social services help at the point of running away, and are a particularly vulnerable and neglected group. It is vital that there is more flexibility within official service provision to support and assist this group of young people. The fact that the enhanced leaving care services laid out in the Children (Leaving Care) Act 2000 only apply to young people who have been accommodated by a local authority for 13 weeks prior to their 16th birthday further excludes this group of young people.

Holistic working approaches

A 'holistic' approach to drug interventions was positively described, both by young people in the sample and members of staff alike. This involved viewing all aspects of the young people's lives, including their health, housing, employment and financial situation, as inter-dependent. It was evident from many of the in-depth interviews that drug using inter-played with many different aspects of their lives. It was only when all of these aspects were addressed that successful transitions were more likely to take place.

This multi-method approach was more appropriate to young people with more problematic drug use. It also suited those with less serious drug using patterns where a change of natural life events provided a positive influence to reduce their drug problems. It avoided giving too high a profile to drug issues. It also focused attention on the wider aspects of young people's complex leaving care transitions, which provide the basis of secure independent living. Drugs were only a small part of the challenges these young people faced on leaving care. Any interventions should be part of more general planning that embraces issues such as housing, employment and training based on a comprehensive needs assessment.

Specialist services

This study has confirmed a lack of appropriate specialist services for young people with drug problems. Whilst the overall numbers of young people who require such interventions are small, it is imperative that specialist services, such as 'detox' facilities are available. For people who develop problematic patterns of drug use, ceasing to use certain drugs can be difficult. When the motivation to give up is reached, it is helpful for the young person to be able to access relevant services and facilities at that point rather than having to wait. Whilst this might be difficult to plan for, enabling a young person to address their drug use before it becomes more developed and longer-term is important (Dorn and South, 1984).

GOLDSMITHS CARE LEAVERS PROJECT

Self-report questionnaire: young people leaving care

This is a questionnaire about you, some of your thoughts, some activities you might be involved in, your use of different substances and your health.

The questionnaire is **private** and confidential, which means that nobody who knows you will ever see it or find out what you have said. Your carers, key workers etc will never know what you have written here. We will not identify you in anything we write.

Questionnaire code

Site code (where recruited)

Local authority code

Care status

First some questions about you

1. Are you male or female? (Please tick which).

Male	Female

2. When were you born? (Date of birth).

Month	Year

3. Which of the following best describes you? (Please tick one).

White		Chinese	
Black		Mixed race	
Asian		**Other (specify)**	

4. What type of accommodation are you currently living in? (Please tick one)

Bed and breakfast	
Supported housing	
Own flat (I live alone)	
Own flat (I live with my partner/friends/family)	
Residential care unit	
Foster family	
Hostel	
Bed sit	
Other (please specify)	

5.   I am currently (tick which one applies to you).

Attending school	
Attending college	
School excluded (permanently)	
On a training scheme	
Attending a special education unit	
Unemployed	
Employed (what do you do?)	
Claiming sickness or disability benefit	
Doing nothing	
Other (please specify)	

6.   What is the highest form of qualification you have? (Tick which one applies to you).

A Level's	
GCSE's	
NVQ	
None	
Other training (please specify)	

These next questions are about living in care

7.   How long ago did you leave care, by this we mean your last foster placement or placement in a residential unit? This does not include supported lodgings. **(If still in care go to Q. 9)**.

Years	Months

8.   How long were you in care?

Years	Months

Now go to Q. 11

9.   How long have you been living in care?

Years	Months

10.   If you are still in care, approximately when will you be leaving?

Years	Months

11.   How long have you been living where you are at the moment?

Years	Months

12.   Since leaving care, that is your last foster care placement or placement in a residential unit, how many different places (i.e. hostels, supported lodgings etc) have you lived?
(If still in care, go to Q. 13)

I have lived in	different places since leaving care

13.   How many different care homes/units have you lived in?
(Write **0 0** if you have not lived in a care home/unit).

I have lived in	care homes

14.   How many different foster families have you lived with?
(Write **0 0** if you have not lived with a foster family).

I have lived with	foster families

15.   Have you ever lived in a local authority secure unit or Young Offenders Institution?

Yes	No
Yes	No

If no, please go to Q.19

16. On how many separate occasions have you lived in a local authority secure unit or Young Offenders Institution?

On	separate occasions

17. On the last occasion you lived in a local authority secure unit or YOI, how long were you in for?

Years	Months

18. Upon leaving the last secure unit or YOI you were in, where did you go to live after that? **(Please tick one)**

Bed and breakfast	
Supported housing	
Own flat	
Residential care unit	
Foster family	
Own family	
Bed sit	
Hostel	
Other (please specify)	

19. When did you last live with a parent or other member of your family (i.e. aunty, uncle, grandmother, brother, sister) for an extended period?

Years and	months ago

20. Who was it with? (tick all that apply).

Mother	
Father	
Stepfather	
Stepmother	
Aunty	
Uncle	
Grandmother	
Grandfather	
Brother/s	
Sisters/s	
Other (please specify)	

21. Who of your family are you in regular contact with? (tick all which apply).

Mother	
Father	
Stepfather	
Stepmother	
Aunty	
Uncle	
Grandmother	
Grandfather	
Brother/s	
Sisters/s	
No one	
Other (please specify)	

22. How many children of your own do you have? (**If none, please go to Q.23**).

None	
One	
Two	
Other (how many?)	

23. Where do your children live at the moment?

With me	
With me and my partner	
With their mother/father	
With their grandparents	
They are in care	
Other (please specify)	

Now some questions about cigarette smoking

24. Which one of these statements best describes you? **(Tick ONE box only)**.

I have never tried a cigarette not even a puff	
I have tried smoking cigarettes, but I don't smoke now	
I smoke cigarettes, but less than once a week	
I smoke cigarettes at least once a week	
I smoke cigarettes every day	

25. How old were you when you first smoked a cigarette? (if you have never smoked, put **00**).

years of age

26. On the last day you smoked (apart from today) how many cigarettes did you have? If you have never smoked write **0**, if you cannot remember write **DK**.

I smoked	cigarettes last time

The next questions are about drinking alcohol
(e.g. beer, lager, wine, hooch, vodka etc.)

Remember nobody here will ever know what you have written.

27.   Which one of these statements best describes you? **(Tick ONE box only)**.

I have never tried an alcoholic drink (not even a sip)	
I have tried drinking alcohol, but I don't drink now	
I drink alcohol but only on special occasions (e.g. Xmas, New Year or at parties)	
I drink alcohol but less than once a month	
I drink alcohol at least once a month	
I drink alcohol at least once a week	
I drink alcohol most days	

28.   How old were you when you first started to drink regularly? If you have never had alcoholic drinks then put **00**.

Years old

29.   How much would you be likely to drink in a typical drinking session? **(Tick which one applies to you)**.

No drinks	
1-2 drinks	
More than 2 but less than 5	
5 drinks or more	

30.   What do you usually drink?

Lager	
Beer	
Cider	
Spirits	
Wine	
Alco-pops	
Other (please specify)	

31.   How often do you get drunk? **(Please tick one)**.

Never	
Occasionally	
Once a week	
3-4 times a week	
Everyday	

The next questions are about drugs

Remember nobody you know will ever know what you have written.

32.   Looking at the lists below please indicate which drugs you have used. Tick any you have used. Next write in how old you were when you first used.

	Ever used	How old when First used
Speed/amphetamine (whizz, uppers, sulph)		
Cannabis (marijuana, puff, hash, ganga, blow, draw)		
Cocaine (Charlie, coke)		
Crack/rock		
Ecstasy (E, pills, sweeties)		
Heroin (smack, brown, junk, skag)		
LSD (acid, trips)		
Magic mushrooms (mushies, shrooms)		
Ketamine (Special K)		
Methadone/physeptone		
Semeron		
Tranquillisers not prescribed by a doctor (jellies, wobbly, eggs, Tranx, temazepam, valium, benzos)		
Poppers, nitrites (rush, amyl nitrate, butyl nitrate)		
Anabolic steroids		
Solvents to sniff or inhale (gas, glue, aerosols, lighter fluids)		
Pills unknown		
NONE OF THESE **(if this box is ticked, please go to Q.46)**		

33. Here we want you to tell us how often you use the following drugs. (Please tick **all** boxes which apply).

	Last year	Last month	Last week	Most days
Speed/amphetamine (whizz, uppers, sulph)				
Cannabis (marijuana, puff, hash, ganga, blow, draw)				
Cocaine (Charlie, coke)				
Crack/rock				
Ecstasy (E, pills, sweeties)				
Heroin (smack, brown, junk, skag)				
LSD (acid, trips)				
Magic mushrooms (mushies, shrooms)				
Ketamine (Special K)				
Methadone/physeptone				
Semeron				
Tranquillisers not prescribed by a doctor (jellies, wobbly, eggs, Tranx, temazepam, valium, benzos)				
Poppers, nitrites (rush, amyl nitrate, butyl nitrate)				
Anabolic steroids				
Solvents to sniff or inhale (gas, glue, aerosols, lighter fluids)				
Pills unknown				

The next few questions are more specifically about your drug use

They may not seem relevant to you but please assist us by answering them all. Remember your answers are confidential. Nobody you know will know what you have written.

34. Do you have a favourite drug you use?

Yes	No

35. Do you ever use drugs alone?

Yes	No

36.   Do you use drugs because you're bored, lonely or anxious?

Yes	No

37.   Do you think a lot about drugs and drug use?

Yes	No

38.   Do you need to use more and more drugs to get high?

Yes	No

39.   Do you feel irritable or anxious if you don't use drugs?

Yes	No

40.   Do you miss your favourite drug if you don't use it for a while?

Yes	No

The next questions are about drug injection

41.   Have you ever injected any drugs? **(If no, go to Q.46)**.

Yes	No

42.   If yes, please list what drug(s) you have injected and how old you were when you first injected them.

Drugs injected	Age when first injected

43.   How often do you inject drugs?

I have tried it just once	
A few times more than 6 months ago	
A few times recently	
More than 10 times	

44. Have you ever shared any injecting equipment (i.e. needles, syringes etc)?

Yes	No

45. On the last occasion you injected and shared equipment, who did you share with? (Please tick).

I have NEVER shared equipment	
I have shared with friends my own age	
I have shared with older friends	
Shared with a girlfriend/boyfriend	
Shared with family members	
Shared with someone I knew of	
Shared with a stranger	

46. For each of the following drugs, how harmful do you think each one is? (Tick the relevant box).

Drugs	Very harmful	Fairly harmful	Not very harmful	Not at all harmful	Don't know
Cannabis					
E's					
Speed					
Cocaine					
Heroin					
Tobacco					
Alcohol					

The next few questions are about when you were growing up

47. When you were growing up/living at home, how often did your parent/s drink?

	Everyday	3-4 times p/wk	Once a week	Occasionally	Never	Don't know
Mother						
Father						

48.   In relation to the previous question, how would you describe their drinking patterns?

	Light drinker	Moderate drinker	Heavy drinker	Other (please specify)
Mother				
Father				

49.   When you were growing up/living at home did any members of your family use any drugs? If yes, please tick all that apply and state what type of drugs they used. If you don't know write **D K**.

	Used drugs	They used
Mother		
Stepmother		
Father		
Stepfather		
Sister		
Brother		
Nobody used		
Other (please specify)		

The next few questions are about any drug problems and any treatment for these problems that you may have had

50.   Have you ever experienced any problems that were related to using drugs? **(If ticked no, please go to Q.52)**.

Yes	No

51. *If yes, what were the problems to do with? (tick any boxes below which apply).*

Health	
Money	
Friends	
Family	
Care Staff	
Foster Parents	
Homelessness	
Police	
School	
Other (please specify)	

Please describe in more detail

52. Have you ever received medical attention or been in treatment for any alcohol or drug related problems you have had?

	For drugs	For alcohol
Yes		
No		

53. If you have had any drug or alcohol related problems, on the last occasion, who did you get help or treatment from? (tick any which apply).

	For drugs	For alcohol
My doctor		
Hospital (A & E)		
Drugs Counsellor		
Drugs Service		
Secure Unit Detox		
Other (please specify)		

54.   Thinking back over the last year, how would you describe your drinking?

I drink a bit less than I used to	
I drink a lot less than I used to	
My drinking has remained the same	
I drink a lot more than I used to	
I drink a bit more than I used to	
I have stopped drinking altogether	
I have never drunk alcohol **(go to Q. 56)**	

55.   If there have been any changes to your alcohol intake over the last year, what have these been related to?

56.   Thinking back over the last year, how would you describe your drug use?

I have stopped taking drugs	
I use drugs a lot more frequently now	
I use drugs a bit more frequently now	
I use drugs a lot less frequently than I used to	
I use drugs a bit less frequently than I used to	
My drug use has remained the same	
I have never taken any drugs	

57.   If your drug use has changed over the last year, what would you say this has been related to?

The following questions are about your health

58.   How would you describe your health? (Tick which one applies to you).

Excellent	
Very good	
Good	
Fair	
Poor	

59.   If you have responded **fair** or **poor**, what is the main reason?

60.   Do you have any illnesses (e.g. asthma, diabetes)?

Yes	No

61.   If yes, what are they?

62.   Are you currently taking any prescribed medication?

Yes	No

63. Why are you currently being prescribed medication?

64. How long ago did you last visit a doctor or medical expert?

65. What was this visit related to?

66. If there is anything else you would like to say then write it in the space below. Thank you for your time in taking part.

Appendix B   Themes for follow-up interviews

Interviews will be semi-structured around a cluster of themes, with a focus on recent events, experiences and changes since the questionnaire interview. All interviews will be with people who reported that they used drugs at questionnaire stage, or with a history of drug use.

The interview will begin with an open-ended question to allow the young person initially to define their experiences in their own terms: "What's been going on in your life for the past x months since we met?"

The following themes will then be pursued and prompted:

- Accommodation. Any periods of homelessness? Or staying with friends etc?

- Employment/education/training position

- Financial situation

- Friends

- Family links

- Dependants i.e. children dependent siblings, parents etc.

- Contacts with agencies, social services, housing department, etc.

- Experiences with drugs

- Types of formal and informal help?

Appendix C

Question structure for interviewing leaving care team staff

Staff status:
- When did you start working in care?
- How long have you worked in care/with care leavers/here?
- What was your background before?
- Are you a live-in member of staff here?

Frequency of drug use:
- What's your perception of drug use amongst the young people coming through the unit? (Ranging from mild use through to major users)
- Does young people's drug use come up on a day-to-day basis in your work?
- Do you think drugs come into the unit at all? How regularly, on what kind of basis?

Types of drug using:
- How would you define a problematic user? How heavy is the use?
- Are there any categories of young people that you think are more vulnerable/prone to certain types of drug use? (e.g. certain age bands? girls/boys? certain areas?)
- If some of the young people are using, does it have a ripple effect on the other residents? i.e. do the young people tend to be easily influenced by peers when it comes to drug taking?
- Have you seen any drug taking patterns develop among the young people?

Staff/ young people interactions:
- How is suspected drug use detected? (e.g. do you act on suspicion?)
- And dealt with by staff? What's the staff policy on drug use amongst the young people?
- Have you ever faced tension with having to call the police? Do the police help?
- How does young people's drug use affect relationships with staff, in terms of the young people's behaviour and treatment of staff?

- Do you personally have different attitudes towards different types of drugs and patterns of drug taking?
- Do you feel adequately knowledgeable and equipped to deal with young people using drugs and whatever else is presented to you relating to drug use?

Young people's perceptions of and attitudes towards drugs:
- Are the young people open about discussing drugs?
- Do you find them to be moralistic about drug use? Why do you think so/not?
- Do you think they know about the dangers and health risks involved?
- Do you think there is any bravado when discussing drug use?
- What's the young people's attitudes to different types of drugs?

References

Advisory Council on the Misuse of Drugs (1998) *Drug Misuse and the Environment*. London: Stationery Office.

Ashton, M. (1999) 'Between two stools: children, drugs policy and professional practice', in Marlow, A. and Pearson, G. (eds.) *Young People, Drugs and Community Safety*. Lyme Regis: Russell House, 24-50.

Bedell, G. (2001) 'My Mum didn't look for me'. *The Observer*, November 11.

Biehal, N., Clayden, J., Stein, M. and Wade, J. (1995) *Moving On: Young People and Leaving Care Schemes*. London: HMSO.

Biernacki, P. (1986) *Pathways from Heroin Addiction: Recovery Without Treatment*. Philadelphia: Temple University Press.

Blyth, E. (2001) 'The impact of the first term of the new Labour Government on social work in Britain: the interface between education policy and social work'. *British Journal of Social Work*, 31, 563-577.

Bradford, S. and Urquhart, C. (1998) 'The making and breaking of young men: suicide and the adolescent male'. *Youth and Policy*, 61, 28-41.

Broad, B. (1999) 'Young people leaving care: moving towards 'joined up' solutions?' *Children and Society*, 13, 81-93.

Buchanan, A. (1999) 'Are care leavers significantly dissatisfied and depressed in adult life?' *Adoption and Fostering*, 23, 4, 35-40.

Bullock, R., Gooch, D. and Little, M. (1998) *Children Going Home: the Reunification of Families*. Aldershot, Ashgate.

Collins, M. E. (2001) 'Transition to adulthood for vulnerable youths: a review of research and implications for policy'. *Social Service Review*, 75, 2, 271-291.

Colton, M., Aldgate, J. and Heath, A. (1991) Behavioural problems among children in and out of care. *Social Work and Social Sciences Review, 2,* 177-91.

Department of Health (1998) *UNICEF Report: A League Table of Teenage Births in Rich Nations.* London: SO.
Http://www.doh.gov.uk/teenagepregnancyunit

Department of Health (1999) *Me Survive, Out There.* London: SO.

Department of Health (2000) *Children (Leaving Care) Act 2000.* London: Department of Health.

Department of Health (2002) *Children Looked After by Local Authorities Year Ending 31st March 2001, England.* London: Department of Health Statistical Bulletin.

Department of Health (2001) *Consultation on Young Runaways. Background Paper by the Social Exclusion Unit.* London: SO.

Donoghue, M., Dorn, N., James, C., Jones, S., Ribbens, J. and South, N. (1987) 'How families and communities respond to heroin', in N. Dorn and N. South (Eds.). *A Land Fit for Heroin? Drug Policies, Prevention and Practice.* London: Macmillan, 95-124.

Dorn, N. and South, N. (1984) *Helping Drug Users.* Aldershot: Gower.

Dorn, N., Ribbens, J. and South, N. (1987) *Coping With a Nightmare: Family Feelings About Long-Term Drug Use.* London: ISDD.

Economic and Social Research Council (2002) *Research Programme on Youth, Citizenship and Social Change.*
http://www.tsa.uk.com/YCSC/index.html

Evans, K. and Alade, S. (2000) *Vulnerable Young People and Drugs: Opportunities to Tackle Inequalities.* London: DrugScope.

Health Education Authority (1999) *Drug Use in England. Results of the 1996 National Drugs Campaign Survey.* London: Health Education Authority.

Foster, K., Wilmot, A., and Dobbs, J. (1990) *General Household Survey 1988.* London. HMSO.

Foxcroft, D. and Lowe, G. (1991) 'Adolescent drinking behaviour and family socialisation factors: a meta-analysis'. *Journal of Adolescence*, 14, 255-73.

Furlong, A. and Cartmel, F. (1997) *Young People and Social Change: Individualization and Risk in Late Modernity*. Buckingham: Open University Press.

Garmezy, N. (1996) 'Reflections and commentary on risk, resilience and development', in Haggerty, R., Sherrod, L., Garmezy, N. and Rutter, M. (eds.) *Stress, Risk and Resilience in Children and Adolescents: Processes, Mechanisms and Interventions*. Cambridge: Cambridge University Press, 1-18.

Goulden, C. and Sondhi, A. (2001) *At the Margins: Drug Use by Vulnerable Young People in the 1998/9 Youth Lifestyles Survey*. Home Office Research Study 228. London: Home Office.

Hagan, J. and McCarthy, B. (1998) *Mean Streets: Youth Crime and Homelessness*. Cambridge: Cambridge University Press.

Health Advisory Service (2001) *The Substance of Young Needs: Review 2001*. London: Health Advisory Service.

Hendricks, J. (1989) The health needs of young people in care. *Adoption and Fostering*, 13, 43-50.

Home Office (2002) *Drug Seizure and Offender Statistics, United Kingdom, 2000*. Home Office Statistical Bulletin 4/02. London: Home Office.

Lewis, H. (2000) 'Children in public care: overcoming barriers to effective mental health care'. *Young Minds*, 46, 16-18.

Lowe, G., Foxcroft, D. R. and Sibley, D. (1993) *Adolescent Drinking and Family Life*. Reading: Harwood Academic Press.

Marsh, A., Dobbs, J. and White, A. (1986) *Adolescent Drinking*. London: HMSO.

Mayer, J. E. and Timms, N. (1970) *The Client Speaks: Working Class Impressions of Casework*. London: Routledge.

McCann, J., James, A., Wilson S. and Dunn, G. (1996) Prevalence of psychiatric disorders in young people in the care system. *British Medical Journal*, 313, 1529-30.

Measham, F., Parker, H. and Aldridge, J. (1998) *Starting, Switching, Slowing and Stopping: Report for the Drugs Prevention Initiative Integrated Programme*. Home Office Paper 21. London: Home Office.

Miller, P. and Plant, M. (1996) Drinking, smoking and illicit drug use among 15 and 16-year-olds in the United Kingdom. *British Medical Journal*, 313, 394-7.

Needle, R., McCubbin, H., Wilson, M. and Reineck, R. (1986) 'Interpersonal influences in adolescent drug use: the role of older siblings, parents and peers'. *International Journal of the Addictions*, 21, 739-766.

Newburn, T. and Shiner, M. (2001) *Teenage Kicks? Young People and Alcohol: A Review of the Literature*. York: Joseph Rowntree Foundation.

Newburn, T., Ward, J. and Pearson, G. (2002) *Drug Use Among Young People in Care*. Youth Citizenship and Social Change Research Briefing. (in press).

Parker, H. (2000) 'How young Britons obtain their drugs: drugs transactions at the point of consumption', in Natarajan, M. and Hough, M. (eds.) *Illegal Drug Markets: From Research to Prevention Policy*. Monsey, NY: Criminal Justice Press, 59-81.

Parker, H., Aldridge, J. and Measham, F. (1998) *Illegal Leisure: The Normalisation of Adolescent Recreational Drug Use*. London: Routeledge.

Pearson, G. and Shiner, M. (2002) 'Rethinking the generation gap: attitudes to illicit drugs among young people and adults'. *Criminal Justice*, 2, 71-86.

Pearson, G. and Hobbs, D. (2001) *Middle Market Drug Distribution*. Home Office Research Study 227. London: Home Office.

Pearson, G. (2001) 'Normal drug use: ethnographic fieldwork among an adult network of recreational drug users in inner London', *Substance Use and Misuse*, 36, 1 and 2, 167-200.

Pearson, G. (2000) 'Substance Abuse and the Family'. *Current Opinion in Psychiatry*, 13, 305-308.

Pearson, G., Gilman, M. and McIver, S. (1985) *Young People and Heroin: An Examination of Heroin Use in the North of England.* London: Health Education Council.

Plant, M.A., Bagnell, G. and Foster, J. (1990) 'Teenage heavy drinkers: alcohol related knowledge, beliefs, experiences, motivation and the social context of drinking'. *Alcohol and Alcoholism,* 25, 691-698.

Plant, M. and Plant, M. (1992) *Risk Takers. Alcohol, Drugs, Sex and Youth.* London: Tavistock, Routledge.

Plant, M.A., Peck, D, F. and Samuel, E. (1985) *Alcohol, Drugs and School Leavers.* London: Tavistock.

Police Foundation (2000) *Drugs and the Law. Report of the Independent Inquiry into the Misuse of Drugs Act 1971.* London: Police Foundation.

President of the Council (1998) *Tackling Drugs to Build a Better Britain.* Cm. 3945. London: HMSO.

Ramsay, M., Baker, P., Goulden, C., Sharp, C. and Sondhi, A. (2001) *Drug Misuse Declared in 2000: Results from the British Crime Survey.* Home Office Research Study 224. London: Home Office.

Ramsay, M. and Partridge, S. (1999) *Drug Misuse Declared in 1998: Results from the British Crime Survey.* Home Office Research Study 197. London: Home Office.

Ramsay, M. and Spiller, J. (1997) *Drug Misuse Declared: Results from the 1996 British Crime Survey.* London: Home Office Research Study 172. London: Home Office.

Rutter, M., Giller, H. and Hagell, A. (1998) *Antisocial Behaviour by Young People.* Cambridge: Cambridge University Press.

Saunders, L. and Broad, B. (1997) 'The health needs of young people leaving care' cited in Lewis, H. (2000).

SCODA (1997) *Drug-related Early Intervention: Developing Services for Young People and Families.* London: SCODA.

Shiner, M. and Newburn, T. (1997) 'Definitely, Maybe Not? The Normalisation of Recreational Drug Use Amongst Young People' *Sociology*, 31, 3, 511-529.

Social Exclusion Unit (2001) *Consultation on Young Runaways* Report. London: SEU.

Social Services Inspectorate (1997) *Substance Misuse and Young People*. London: Department of Health.

Swadi, H. (1997) 'Substance misuse in adolescence questionnaire (SMAQ): a pilot study of a screening instrument for problematic use of drugs and volatile substances in adolescents'. *Child Psychology and Psychiatry Review*, 2, 63-67.

Swadi, H. and Zeitlin, H. (1988) 'Peer influence and adolescent substance abuse: a promising side?' *British Journal of Addiction*, 83, 153-158.

Valios, N. (2001) 'The opening of a new chapter for care leavers'. *Community Care*, 30 August, 30-31.

Vernon, J. (2000) *Audit and Assessment of Leaving Care Services in London*. National Children's Bureau: Department of Health.

Waldorf, D., Reinarman, C. and Murphy, S. (1991) *Cocaine Changes: The Experience of Using and Quitting*. Philadelphia: Temple University Press.

Ward, J. (1998) 'Substance use among young people 'looked after' by social services'. *Drugs: Education, Prevention and Policy*, 5, 3, 257-267.

Williams, J. H., Ayers, C. D., Abbott, R. D., Hawkins, J. D. and Catalano, R. F. (1999) 'Racial differences in risk factors for delinquency and substance use among adolescents'. *Social Work Research*, 23, 4, 241-256.

Willner, P. (2000) 'Further validation and development of a screening instrument for the assessment of substance misuse in adolescents'. *Addiction*, 95, 11, 1691-1698.

Wills, T., Sandy, J., Yaeger, A. and Shinar, O. (2001) 'Family risk factors and adolescence substance misuse: moderation effects for temperament dimensions'. *Developmental Psychology*, 37, 3, 283-297.

Requests for Publications

Copies of our publications and a list of those currently available may be obtained from:

Home Office
Research, Development and Statistics Directorate
Communication Development Unit
Room 275, Home Office
50 Queen Anne's Gate
London SW1H 9AT
Telephone: 020 7273 2084 (answerphone outside of office hours)
Facsimile: 020 7222 0211
E-mail: publications.rds@homeoffice.gsi.gov.uk

alternatively

why not visit the RDS web-site at
          Internet: http://www.homeoffice.gov.uk/rds/index.htm

where many of our publications are available to be read on screen or downloaded for printing.